The
Glad Tidings

By
E. J. Waggoner

TEACH Services, Inc.
Brushton, New York

Copyright © 1997 TEACH Services, Inc.

ISBN 1-57258-108-5
Library of Congress Catalog Card No. 97-60505

Published by

TEACH Services, Inc.
RR 1, Box 182
Brushton, New York 12916

Contents

Preface

The Epistle to the Galatians, together with its companion, the Epistle to the Romans, was the source, through the Spirit, of the Reformation of the sixteenth century, the key-note of which was, "The just shall live by faith." The reformation then begun is not yet complete, and the same watchword needs to be sounded now as then. If the people of God will become filled with the truth so vividly set forth in this epistle, both the church and the world will be stirred as profoundly as in the days of Luther. May this speedily be the case, and thus the times of restoration of all things be hastened! {7}

THE GLAD TIDINGS

It is quite common, in writing upon any book in the Bible, to spend some time on an "Introduction" to the book in question—setting forth the nature of it, the circumstances under which it was written, and the probable purpose of the writer, together with many other things, partly conjectural, and partly derived from the book itself. All such statements the reader has to take on the authority of the one making them, since, not having yet studied the book, he can not judge for himself. The best way is to introduce him at once to the study of the book, and then he will, if diligent and faithful, soon learn all that it has to reveal concerning itself. We learn more of a man by talking with him than by hearing somebody talk about him. So we will proceed at once to the study of the Epistle to the Galatians, and let it speak for itself.

Nothing can take the place of the Scriptures themselves. If all would study the Bible as prayerfully and as conscientiously as they ought, giving earnest heed to every word, and receiving it as coming directly from God, there would be no need of any other {8} religious book. Whatever is written should be for the purpose of calling people's attention more sharply to the words of Scripture; whatever substitutes any man's opinions for the Bible, so that by it people are led to rest content without any further study of the Bible itself, is worse than useless. The reader is, therefore, most earnestly urged to study, first of all, the Scripture text very diligently and carefully, so that every reference to it will be a reference to a familiar acquaintance. May God grant that this little aid to the study of the Word may make every reader better acquainted with all Scripture, which is able to make him wise unto salvation. {9}

The Revelation Of Jesus Christ, The Real Gospel

"PAUL, an apostle (not from men, neither through man, but through Jesus Christ, and God the Father, who raised Him from the dead), and all the brethren which are with me, unto the churches of Galatia: Grace to you and peace from God the Father, and our Lord Jesus Christ, who gave Himself for our sins, that He might deliver us out of this present evil world, according to the will of our God and Father; to whom be the glory forever and ever. Amen.

"I marvel that ye are so quickly removing from Him that called you in the grace of Christ unto a different gospel; which is not another gospel; only there are some that trouble you, and would pervert the Gospel of Christ. But though we, or an angel from heaven, should preach unto you any gospel other than that which we preached unto you, let him be anathema. As we have said before, so say I now again, If any man preacheth unto you any gospel other than that which ye received, let him be anathema. For am I now persuading men, or God? or am I seeking to please men? if I were still pleasing men, I should not be a servant of Christ.

"For I make known to you, brethren, as touching the Gospel which was preached by me, that it is not after man. For neither did I receive it from man, {10} nor was I taught it, but it came to me through revelation of Jesus Christ. For ye have heard of my manner of life in time past in the Jews' religion, how that beyond measure I persecuted the church of God, and made havoc of it; and I advanced in the Jews' religion beyond many of mine own age among my countrymen, being more exceedingly zealous for the traditions of my fathers. But when it was the good pleasure of God, who separated me, even from my mother's womb, and called me through His grace, to reveal His Son in me, that I might preach Him among the Gentiles; immediately I conferred not with flesh and blood; neither went I up to Jerusalem to them which were apostles before me; but I went away into Arabia; and again I returned unto Damascus.

"Then after three years I went up to Jerusalem to visit Cephas, and tarried with him fifteen days. But other of the apostles saw I none, save James the Lord's brother. Now touching the things which I write unto you, behold, before God, I lie not. Then I came into the regions of Syria and Cilicia. And I was still unknown by face unto the churches of Judea which were in Christ; but they only heard say, He that once persecuted us now preacheth the faith of which he once made havoc; and they glorified God in me." Galatians 1, R.V.

An Apostolic Salutation

The first five verses form a greeting such as, with the exception of the first verses of the book of Romans, is not to be found elsewhere in the Bible, and, consequently, nowhere else in the world. {11}

It contains the whole Gospel. If there were no other portion of Scripture accessible, this contains sufficient to save the world.

If we would study this small portion as diligently, and prize it as highly, as if there were no more, we should find our faith and hope and love infinitely strengthened, and our knowledge of the rest of the Bible much increased. In reading it, let the Galatians sink out of sight, and let each one consider it the voice of God, through His apostle, speaking to him to-day.

A Good Commission

An apostle is one who is sent. Paul was an apostle of Jesus Christ, and of God, the Father, who raised Him from the dead. He had good backing. A messenger's confidence is in proportion to the authority of the one who sends him, and to his confidence in that authority and power. Paul knew that he was sent by the Lord, and he knew that the power of God is the power that raises from the dead. Now "he whom God hath sent speaketh the words of God." John 3:34. Thus it was that Paul spoke with authority, and the words which he spoke were the commandments of God. 1 Cor. 14:37. So in reading this epistle, or any other in the Bible, we have not to make allowance for the writer's personal peculiarities and prejudices. It is true that each writer retains his own individuality, since God chooses different men to do different work solely on account of their different personality; but it is God's Word in all, and nothing need be taken off from the authority of the message, and set down to the score of prejudice or early education. {12}

It is well to remember that not only the apostles, but every one in the church, is commissioned to "speak as the oracles of God." 1 Pet. 4:11. All who are in Christ are new creatures, having been reconciled to God by Jesus Christ; and all who have been reconciled are given the word and ministry of reconciliation, so that they are ambassadors for Christ, as though God by them, even as by Christ, was beseeching men to be reconciled to Himself. 2 Cor. 5:17–20. This is a wonderful support against discouragement and against fear to speak God's message. The

ambassadors of earthly governments have authority propor-
tionate to the power of the king or ruler whom they represent;
but Christians represent the King of kings and Lord of lords.

Apostles Are of God

"God hath set some in the church, first apostles, secondarily
prophets, thirdly teachers, after that miracles, then gifts of
healings," etc. 1 Cor. 12:28. Let it be borne in mind that all these
are set in the church by God Himself. No other can do it. It is
impossible for men to make a true apostle or prophet. There are
certain people in the world who say to others, Why do you not
have apostles and prophets, etc., in the church? ignoring the
fact that God has them in His church until this day, although
they are often unrecognized, even as the apostleship of Paul and
the others was often denied. Then there are some combinations
of people who claim to have all these among them. Reading that
God has set them in the church, they see that the true church
of God ought to have apostles, prophets, etc. Accordingly {13}
they appoint some to be apostles, others to be prophets, and
others to be teachers, and then they point to these as evidence
that they are the true church of God. The fact is, however, that
this is the strongest possible proof that they are not the church
of God. If they were the church of God, apostles and prophets
would be set among them by God Himself; but the fact that they
themselves are obliged to make apostles and prophets, shows
that they have none in fact. They are simply setting up a dummy
to hide the absence of the reality; but the presence of the sham
only emphasizes the absence of the real.

Not of Men

All Gospel teaching is based upon and derives its authority
from the fact of the Divinity of Christ. The apostles and prophets
were so fully imbued with this truth that it appears everywhere
in their writings. In the very first verse of this epistle we find it
in the statement that Paul was not an apostle of men, nor by any
man, but by Jesus Christ, who is "the image of the invisible God"
(Col. 1:15), "the effulgence of His glory, and the very image of
His substance" (Heb. 1:1–3, R.V.); He was in the beginning with
God, and was God, before the world was. John 1:1; 17:5. "He
is before all things, and in Him all things consist." Col. 1:17,
R.V.

The Father and the Son

"Jesus Christ, and God the Father, who raised Him from the
dead," are associated on equal terms. "I and My Father are
One." John 10:30. They both sit upon one throne. Heb. 1:3; 8:1;
Rev. 3:21. The counsel of peace is between {14} them both.
Zech.6:12,13. Jesus was the Son of God all His life, although

He was of the seed of David according to the flesh; but it was by the resurrection from the dead, which was accomplished by the power of the Spirit of holiness, that His Sonship was demonstrated to all. Rom. 1:3,4. This epistle has the same authority as Paul's apostleship: it is from Him who has power to raise the dead, and from Him who was raised from the dead.

The Churches of Galatia

Galatia was a province in Asia Minor, so called from the fact that it was inhabited by Gauls,—people who came from the country now known as France. They settled in the territory which took its name from them (Gaul-atia—Galatia), in the third century before Christ. They were, of course, pagans, their religion being quite similar to that of the Druids, of Britain. Paul was the one who first preached Christianity to them, as we read in Acts 16:6; 18:23. The country of Galatia also included Iconium, Lystra, and Derbe, which were visited by Paul, with Barnabas, on his first missionary journey. Acts 14.

Grace and Peace Be to You

This is the word of the Lord, let it be remembered, and therefore means more than man's word. The Lord does not deal in empty compliments. His word is substantial; it carries with it the thing which it names. God's word creates, and here we have the very form of the creative word. {15}

God said, "Let there be light; and there was light," and so on through the whole creation, "He spake, and it was." So here, "Let there be grace and peace to you," and so it is. "The grace of God hath appeared, bringing salvation to all men." Titus 2:11. "Peace I leave with you, My peace I give unto you; not as the world giveth, give I unto you." John 14:27. "Peace, peace to him that is afar off, and to him that is near, saith the Lord." Is. 57:19. God has sent grace and peace, bringing righteousness and salvation to all men—even to you, whoever you are, and to me. When you read this third verse of the first chapter of Galatians, do not read it as a sort of complimentary phrase,—as a mere passing salutation to open the real matter at hand,—but as the creative word that brings to you personally all the blessings of the peace of God, that passeth all understanding. It is to us the same word that Jesus spoke to the woman: "Thy sins are forgiven." "Go in peace." Luke 7:48–50. Peace is given to you; therefore, "let the peace of God rule in your hearts."

The Gift of Christ

This grace and peace come from Christ, "who gave Himself for our sins." "Unto every one of us is given grace according to the measure of the gift of Christ." Eph. 4:7. But this grace is "the grace that is in Christ Jesus." 2 Tim. 2:1. Therefore we know that Christ Himself is given to every one of us. The fact that men live is an evidence that Christ has been given to them, for Christ is "the life," and the life is the light of men, and this life-light "lighteth every man that cometh into the world." {16}

John 1:4,9; 14:6. In Christ all things consist (Col. 1:17), and thus it is that since God "spared not His own Son, but delivered Him up for us all," He can not do otherwise than, with Him, freely "give us all things." Rom. 8:32. "His Divine power hath given unto us all things that pertain unto life and godliness." 2 Pet. 1:3. The whole universe is given to us in Christ, and the fullness of the power that is in it is ours for the overcoming of sin. God counts each soul of as much value as all creation. Christ has, by the grace of God, tasted death for every man (Heb. 2:9), so that every man in the world has received the "unspeakable gift" (2 Cor. 9:15). "The grace of God, and the gift by grace, which is by one Man, Jesus Christ, hath abounded unto many," even to all; for "as by the offense of one judgment came upon all men to condemnation; even so by the righteousness of One the free gift came upon all men unto justification of life." Rom. 5:15,18.

Christ Not Divided

The question is asked, "Is Christ divided? was Paul crucified for you?" (1 Cor. 1:13), the answer obviously being in the negative. In that Christ is given to every man, each person gets the whole of Him. The love of God embraces the whole world, but it also singles out each individual. A mother's love is not divided up among her children, so that each one receives only a third, a fourth, or a fifth of it; each one is the object of all her affection. How much more so with the God whose love is more perfect than any mother's, and who Himself is love! {17}

Is. 49:15. Christ is the light of the world, the Sun of Righteousness. But light is not divided among a crowd of people.

If a room full of people be brilliantly lighted, each individual gets the benefit of all the light, just as much as though he were alone in the room. So the life of Christ lights every man that comes into the world, and in every believing heart Christ dwells in all His fullness. Sow a seed in the ground, and you get many seeds, each one having as much life as the one sown. So Christ, the true Seed, whence everything of worth comes, gives to all the whole of His life.

Our Sins Purchased

Christ "gave Himself for our sins." That is to say, He bought them, and paid the price for them. This is a simple statement of fact; the language used is that commonly employed in referring to purchases. "How much did you give for it?" or, "How much do you want for it?" are frequent questions. When we hear a man say that he gave so much for a certain thing, what do we at once know?—We know that that thing belongs to him, because he has bought it. So when the Holy Spirit tells us that Christ gave Himself for our sins, of what should we be equally sure?—That He has bought our sins, and that they belong to Him, and not to us. They are ours no longer, and we have no right to them. Every time we sin we are robbing the Lord, for we must remember that Christ has purchased not merely the specific acts of sin that we have committed, and that are in the past, but the sins that are in us, and which break forth. In this faith there is righteousness. {18}

He Has Bought Us, Too

This follows from the fact that He has purchased our sins, to deliver us from ourselves. Our sins are part of ourselves; nay, they are the whole of us, for our natural lives are nothing but sin. Therefore, Christ could not buy our sins without buying us also. Of this fact we have many plain statements. He "gave Himself for us, that He might redeem us from all iniquity." Titus 2:14. "Ye are not your own; for ye are bought with a price." 1 Cor. 6:19. "Ye were redeemed, not with corruptible things, with silver or gold, from your vain manner of life handed down from your fathers; but with precious blood, as of a lamb without blemish and without spot, even the blood of Christ." 1 Pet. 1:18,19, R.V.

"Accepted in the Beloved"

How often the Gospel worker hears some one say, "I am so sinful that I am afraid the Lord will not accept me;" and even people who have long professed to be Christians, often mournfully wish that they could be sure of their acceptance with God. Now the Lord has given no ground for any such doubts. The question of acceptance is forever settled by what we have just read. Christ has bought us, together with all our sins, and has paid the price. That shows that He has accepted us. Why does a man go to the shop and buy an article?—Because he wants it. If he has paid the price for it, having examined it so as to know what he was buying, does the merchant worry lest he will not accept it?—Not at all; the merchant knows that it is his business to get {19} the goods to the purchaser as soon as possible. If he does not deliver the goods to the purchaser, he is guilty of fraud. The buyer will not indifferently say, "Well, I have done my part, and if he doesn't care to do his, he need not—that's all; he may keep the things if he wants to." No; he will visit the shop, and say, "Why have you not given me what belongs to me?" He will take vigorous measures to come into possession of his property. Even so it is not a matter of indifference to Jesus whether we surrender ourselves to Him or not. He longs with an infinite yearning for the souls that He has purchased with His own blood. "The Son of man is come to seek and to save that which was lost."

Luke 19:10. God has "chosen us in Him before the foundation of the world," and so "He hath made us accepted in the Beloved." Eph. 1:4–6.

"This Present Evil World"

Christ gave Himself for our sins, "that He might deliver us from this present evil world." He will take from us that which He bought, which is our sinfulness. In so doing, He delivers us from this "present evil world." That shows us that "this present evil world" is nothing but our own sinful selves. It is "the lust of the flesh, and the lust of the eyes, and the pride of life." 1 John. 2:16. We ourselves make all the evil there is in the world. It is man that has made the world evil. "By one man sin entered into the world, and death by sin; and so death passed upon all men, for that all have sinned." Rom. 5:12. We need not try to throw the blame {20} upon somebody else; we ourselves provide all the evil that can possibly injure us.

The story is told of a man whose besetting sin was a violent temper. He would frequently become very angry, but he laid all the blame upon the people with whom he lived, who were so exasperating. Nobody, he declared, could do right among such people. So he resolved, as many others have done, to "leave the world," and become a hermit. He chose a cave in the forest for his dwelling-place, far from any other human habitation. In the morning he took his jug to a spring near by to get water for his morning meal. The rock was moss-grown, and the continual flow of water had made it very slippery. As he set his jug down under the stream, it slid away. He put it back, and again it was driven away. Two or three times was this repeated, and each time the replacing of the jug was done with increasing energy. Finally the hermit's patience was utterly exhausted, and exclaiming, "I'll see if you'll not stay!" he picked the vessel up and set it down with such vehemence that it was broken to pieces. There was nobody to blame but himself, and he had the good sense to see that it was not the world around him but the world inside of him that made him sin. Doubtless very many can recognize some experience of their own in this little story.

Luther, in his monk's cell, whither he had gone to escape from the world, found his sins more grievous than ever. Wherever we go, we carry the world with us; we have it in our hearts and on our backs,—a heavy, crushing load. We find that when we would {21} do good, "evil is present" with us. Rom. 7:21. It is present, always, "this present evil world," until, goaded to despair, we cry out, "O wretched man that I am! who shall deliver me from this body of death?" Even Christ found His greatest temptations in the desert, far away from human habitations. All these things teach us that hermits and monks are not in God's plan. God's people are the salt of the earth; and salt, no matter how good it is, is of no use if shut up in a box; it must be mingled with that which is to be preserved.

Deliverance

That which God has promised, He is "able also to perform." He "is able to do exceeding abundantly above all that we ask or think." Eph. 3:20. He "is able to keep you from falling, and to present you faultless before the presence of His glory with exceeding joy." Jude 24. He gave Himself for our sins, that He might deliver us, and He did not die in vain. Deliverance is ours. Christ was sent "to open the blind eyes, to bring out the prisoners from the prison, and them that sit in darkness out of the prison house." Is. 42:7. Accordingly He cries out to the captives, "Liberty!" To them that are bound He proclaims that the prison doors are open. Is. 61:1. To all the prisoners, He says, "Go forth." Is. 49:9. Each soul may say, if he will, "O Lord, truly I am Thy servant; I am Thy servant, and the son of Thine handmaid; Thou hast loosed my bonds." Ps. 116:16. The thing is true, whether we believe it or not. We are the Lord's servants, even though we stubbornly refuse to serve; for He has bought us; and, having bought us, He {22} has broken every bond that hindered us from serving Him. If we but believe, we have the victory that has overcome the world. 1 John. 5:4, R.V.; John 16:33.

The message to us is that our "warfare is accomplished," our "iniquity is pardoned." Is. 40:2. We have but to shout, as Israel did before Jericho, to see that God has given to us the victory. God "hath visited and redeemed His people." Luke 1:68.

Out of Zion has come the Deliverer, to turn away ungodliness from Jacob. Rom. 11:26. "Thanks be to God, which giveth us the victory through our Lord Jesus Christ."

> *"My sin—oh, the bliss of this glorious thought!—*
> *My sin, not in part, but the whole,*
> *Is nailed to His cross, and I bear it no more,*
> *Praise the Lord, praise the Lord, O my soul!"*

The Will of God

All this deliverance is "according to the will of our God and Father." The will of God is our sanctification. 1 Thess. 4:3. He willeth that all men should be saved, and come to the knowledge of the truth. 1 Tim. 2:4. And He "worketh all things after the counsel of His own will." Eph. 1:11. "What! do you mean to teach universal salvation?" We mean to teach just what the Word of God teaches,—that "the grace of God hath appeared, bringing salvation to all men." Titus 2:11, R.V. God has wrought out salvation for every man, and has given it to him; but the majority spurn it, and throw it away. The Judgment will reveal the fact that full and complete salvation was given to every man, and {23} that the lost have deliberately thrown away their birthright possession. Thus every mouth will be stopped.

The will of God is, therefore, something to rejoice in, and not something to be accepted with a wry face, and merely endured. Even though it involves suffering, it is for our good, and is designed to work "for us a far more exceeding and eternal weight of glory." Rom. 8:28; 2 Cor. 4:17. In the law His will is revealed (Rom. 2:18), and we should, therefore, study it, saying with Christ, "I delight to do Thy will, O My God." Ps. 40:8.

Here is the comfort of knowing the will of God. He wills our deliverance from the bondage of sin; therefore, we can pray with the utmost confidence, and with thanksgiving; for "this is the confidence that we have in Him, that, if we ask anything according to His will, He heareth us; and if we know that He hear us, whatsoever we ask, we know that we have the petitions that we desired of Him." 1 John. 5:14,15. Blessed assurance! Let us ever with glad and humble hearts pray, "Thy will be done in earth, as it is in heaven."

To God Be the Glory

Not simply, "To Him be glory," as in the common version, but "To whom be the glory," as in the Revision. "Thine is the kingdom; and the power, and the glory." All glory is God's, whether men acknowledge it or not. To give Him the glory is not to impart anything to Him, but to recognize a fact. We give Him the glory by acknowledging that His is the power. "It is He that hath made us, {24} and not we ourselves." Ps. 100:3. Power and glory are the same, as we learn from Eph. 1:19,20, which tells us that Christ was raised from the dead by the exceeding greatness of God's power, and from Rom. 6:4, where we learn that "Christ was raised up from the dead by the glory of the Father." Also when Jesus by His wondrous power had turned water to wine, we are told that in the performance of the miracle, He "manifested forth His glory." John 2:11. So when we say that to God is the glory, we are saying that the power is all from Him. We do not save ourselves, for we are "without strength." But God is the Almighty, and He can and does save. If we confess that all glory belongs to God, we shall not be indulging in vainglorious imaginations or boastings, and then will God be glorified in us. "Let your light so shine before men, that they may see your good works, and glorify your Father which is in heaven." Matt. 5:16.

The last proclamation of "the everlasting Gospel,"—that which announces the hour of God's Judgment come,—has for its burden, "Fear God, and give glory to Him;" "and worship Him that made heaven, and earth, and the sea, and the fountains of waters." Rev. 14:6,7. Thus we see that the Epistle to the Galatians, which says, "To Him be the glory," is the setting forth of the everlasting Gospel. And it is emphatically a message for the last days. Let us study it, and heed it, that we may help to hasten the time when "the earth shall be filled with the knowledge of the glory of the Lord, as the waters cover the sea." Hab. 2:14. {25}

A Critical Case

The abruptness with which the apostle plunges into the midst of his subject shows how urgent was the matter that called forth his epistle. His spirit seemed to be on fire, and, seizing his pen, he wrote as only one can write who feels upon his heart the burden of souls about to rush to destruction.

Who Calls Men?

"God is faithful, by whom ye were called unto the fellowship of His Son Jesus Christ our Lord." 1 Cor. 1:9. "The God of all grace, who hath called us unto His eternal glory by Christ Jesus," etc. 1 Pet. 5:10. "The promise is unto you, and to your children, and to all that are afar off, even as many as the Lord our God shall call." Acts 2:39. Those that are near, and those that are afar off, include all that are in the world; therefore, God calls everybody. Not all come, however. "The very God of peace sanctify you wholly; and I pray God your whole spirit and soul and body be preserved blameless unto the coming of our Lord Jesus Christ. Faithful is He that calleth you, who also will do it." 1Thess. 5:23,24. It is God who calls men.

Separating from God

Since the Galatian brethren were separating from Him that had called them, and as God is the one who graciously calls men, it is evident that they were separating from God. Thus we see that it was no slight thing that called forth this epistle. Paul's brethren were in mortal danger, and he could not spend time on compliments, but must needs get at {26} once to the subject, and present it in as clear and direct terms as possible.

It may be well in passing to note an opinion that sometimes obtains, namely, that Paul referred to himself as the one who had called the Galatian brethren, and from whom they were removing. A little thought should convince anybody of the fallacy of this idea. First, consider the positive evidence, a little of which is already noted, that it is God who calls. Remember also that it was Paul himself who said that the apostasy would be the result of men's seeking to draw away disciples after themselves (Acts 20:30); he, as the servant of Christ, would be the last man to draw people to himself. It is true that God uses agents, of whom Paul was one, to call men, but it is God, nevertheless, that calls. "God was in Christ, reconciling the world unto Himself;" we are ambassadors for Christ, so that now it is God beseeching men by us instead of by Christ, to be reconciled to Himself. There may be many mouths, but there is only one voice.

It is a small matter to be joined to or separated from men, but a matter of vital importance to be joined to God. Many seem to think that if they are only "members in good standing" in this or that church, they are secure. But the only thing worth considering is, Am I joined to the Lord, and walking in His truth? If one is joined to the Lord, he will very soon find his place among God's people, for those who are not God's people will not have a zealous, consistent follower of God among them very long. See Is. 66:5; John 9:22,33,34; 15:18–21; {27} 16:1–3; 2 Tim. 3:1–5,12. When Barnabas went to Antioch, he exhorted the brethren that with purpose of heart they would "cleave unto the Lord." Acts 11:22,23. That was all that was necessary. If we do that, we shall certainly be with God's own people.

Without God

Those who were departing from God were "without God in the world," just to the extent that they were removed from Him. But those who are in that condition are Gentiles, or heathen. Eph. 2:11,12. It is evident, therefore, that the Galatian brethren were relapsing into heathenism. It could not be otherwise; for whenever any Christian loses his hold upon God, he inevitably and even unconsciously drops back into the old life from which he had been saved. Each backslider will take up the particular habits to which he was formerly a slave. No more hopeless condition can exist in the world than to be without God.

Another Gospel

The Gospel is "the power of God unto salvation to every one that believeth." Rom. 1:16. God Himself is the power, so that separation from God means separation from the Gospel of Christ, who is the power of God. Nothing can be called a gospel unless it professes to give salvation. That which professes to offer nothing but death, can not be called a gospel. "Gospel" means "joyful news," "good tidings," and a promise of death does not answer that description. In order for any false doctrine to pass as the Gospel, it must pretend to be the way of life;

otherwise it could not {28} deceive men. It is evident, therefore, that the Galatians were being seduced from God, by something that promised them life and salvation, but by a power other than that of God, namely, their own power. This other gospel was solely a human gospel. The question consequently would be, Which is the true Gospel? Is it the one that Paul preached? or the one the other men set forth? Therefore, we see that this epistle must be an emphatic presentation of the true Gospel as distinguished from every false gospel.

No Other Gospel

Just as Jesus Christ is the only power of God, and there is no other name than that of Jesus, given among men, whereby salvation can be obtained, so there can be only one Gospel. "Power belongeth unto God," and to Him alone. See Ps. 62:9–11. A sham is nothing. A mask is not a man. So this other gospel, to which the Galatian brethren were being enticed, was only a perverted gospel, a counterfeit, a sham, and no real gospel at all. Some versions give verses 6 and 7 thus: "I marvel that ye are so soon removed…unto another gospel, although there is not any other." Since there is no other gospel now, there never could have been any other, for God changes not. So the Gospel which Paul preached to the Galatians, as well as to the Corinthians,—"Jesus Christ and Him crucified,"—was the Gospel that was preached by Enoch, Noah, Abraham, Moses, and Isaiah. "To Him give all the prophets witness, that through His name whosoever believeth in Him shall receive remission of sins." Acts 10:43. {29}

"Accursed"

If any man, or even an angel from heaven, should preach any other gospel than that which Paul preached, he would bring himself under a curse. There are not two standards of right and wrong. That which will bring a curse to-day would have produced the same result five thousand years ago. Thus we find that the way of salvation has been exactly the same in every age. The Gospel was preached to Abraham (Gal. 3:8), angels being sent to him; and the prophets preached the Gospel (1 Pet. 1:11,12). But if the Gospel preached by them had been different from that preached by Paul, they would have been accursed.

Why should one be accursed for preaching a different gospel?—Because he is the means of fastening others in the curse, by leading them to trust for their salvation in that which professes to be power, but which is nothing. Since the Galatians were removing from God, it is evident that they were trusting to supposed human power—their own power—for salvation. But no man can save another (Ps. 49:6,7), therefore, "cursed be the man that trusteth in man, and maketh flesh his arm, and whose heart departeth from the Lord." Jer. 17:5. The one who leads men into the curse must, of course, himself be accursed. "Cursed be he that maketh the blind to wander out of the way." Deut. 27:18. If this be so of the one who causes a physically blind man to stumble, how much more must it apply to one who causes a soul to stumble to its eternal ruin! To delude people with a false hope of salvation,—to cause them to put {30} their trust in that which can by no means deliver them,—what could possibly be more wicked? It is to lead people to build their house over the bottomless pit. Well might the apostle deliberately reiterate his anathema. Here, again, we see the gravity of the situation that called forth this epistle.

"An Angel from Heaven"

But is there any danger, any possibility, that an angel from heaven would preach any other than the one, true Gospel?— Most assuredly, although it would not be an angel recently come from heaven. We read of "the angels that sinned" (2 Pet. 2:4), and "kept not their first estate, but left their own habitation" (Jude 6), and that the habitation from which they were cast was heaven (Rev. 12:7–9). Now "Satan himself is transformed into an angel of light. Therefore it is no great thing if his ministers also be transformed as the ministers of righteousness." 2 Cor. 11:14,15. It is they who come professing to be the spirits of the departed, and to bring messages fresh from the realms above (where the departed are not), and preaching invariably "another gospel" than the Gospel of Jesus Christ. Beware of them. "Beloved, believe not every spirit, but try the spirits whether they are of God." 1 John. 4:1. "To the law and to the testimony: if they speak not according to this Word, it is because there is no light in them." Is. 8:20. No one need be deceived, so long as he has God's Word. Nay, it is impossible for anybody to be deceived while he holds to the Word of God. That is a light to the way. {31}

Not Men-Pleasers

It is admitted by churchmen that in the first three centuries the church became leavened with paganism, and that, in spite of reformations, much of paganism still remains. Now this was the result of trying to please men. The bishops thought that they could gain influence over the heathen by relaxing some of the strictness of the principles of the Gospel, which they did, and the result was the corruption of the church. Self-love is always at the bottom of efforts to conciliate and please men. The bishops desired (often, perhaps, without being conscious of it) to draw away disciples after themselves. Acts 20:30. In order to gain the favor of the people, they had to compromise and pervert the truth. This was what was being done in Galatia; men were perverting the Gospel of Christ. But Paul was not of that class; he was seeking to please God, and not men. He was the servant of God, and God was the only one whom he needed to please. He who seeks to please men, is the servant of men, and not of God.

This principle is true in every grade of service. The house-servants or the shop assistants who labor only to please men, will not be faithful servants, for they will do good work only where it will be seen, but will slight any task that can not come under the eye of their employers. So Paul exhorts: "Servants, obey in all things your masters according to the flesh; not with eye service, as men-pleasers; but in singleness of heart, fearing God; and whatsoever ye do, do it heartily, as to the Lord, and not unto men; knowing that of the Lord ye shall receive the reward {32} of the inheritance; for ye serve the Lord Christ." Col. 3:22–24. He who cares for nothing else but to serve and please God, will render the best service to men.

This is a thing that needs to be impressed upon all. Christian workers especially need it. There is a tendency to dull the edge of truth, lest we should lose the favor of some wealthy or influential person. How many have stifled conviction, fearing the loss of money or position! Let every one of us remember this: "If I yet pleased men, I should not be the servant of Christ." But this does not mean that we shall be stern and uncourteous. It does not mean that we willingly offend any. God is good to all. He is kind to the unthankful and the unholy. Jesus went about doing good, speaking words of love and comfort. We are to be soul-winners, and so must have a winning manner; but we are to win souls to God, and, therefore, must exhibit only the attractiveness of the loving, crucified One. We serve Christ by allowing His Spirit to control us.

"Who best
Bear His mild yoke, they serve Him best"

"Not of Man"

Note how this epistle emphasizes the fact that the Gospel is divine, not human. In the first verse the apostle states that he was not sent by man, nor to represent any man. Again he says that he is not anxious to please men, but only Christ; and now it is made very clear that the message he bore was wholly from heaven. By birth and education he was opposed to the Gospel, {33} and when he was converted it was by a voice from heaven. Read the accounts of his conversion in Acts 9:1–22; 22:3–16; 26:9–20. The Lord Himself appeared to him in the way as he was breathing threatening and slaughter against the saints of God.

There are no two persons whose experience in conversion is the same, yet the general principles are the same in all. In effect, every person must be converted just as Paul was. The experience will seldom be so striking, but if it is genuine, it must be a revelation from heaven as surely as Paul's was. "All thy children shall be taught of the Lord." Is. 54:13; John 6:45. "Every man therefore that hath heard, and hath learned of the Father, cometh unto Me."

"The anointing which ye have received of Him abideth in you, and ye need not that any man teach you; but as the same anointing teacheth you of all things, and is truth, and is no lie, and even as it hath taught you, ye shall abide in Him." 1 John. 2:27.

Do not make the mistake of supposing that this does away with the necessity for any human agency in the Gospel. If it did, then the apostles would have been self-condemned, because they were preachers of the Gospel. God has set apostles, prophets, teachers, etc., in the church (1 Cor. 12:28); but it is the Spirit of God that works in all these. "He whom God hath sent speaketh the words of God." John 3:34. Therefore, no matter by whom anybody first hears the truth, he is to receive it as coming direct from heaven. The Holy Spirit enables those who wish to do God's will to tell what is truth as soon as they see or hear it, and they accept it, not on the {34} authority of the man through whom it came to them, but on the authority of the God of truth. We may be as sure of the truth which we hold and teach as the apostle Paul was. But whenever anybody cites the name of some highly-esteemed preacher or doctor of divinity, to justify his belief, or to give it more weight with some person whom he would convince, you may be sure that he himself does not know the truth of what he professes. It may be the truth, but he does not know for himself that it is true. It is everybody's privilege to know the truth (John 8:31,32); and when one holds a truth directly from God, ten thousand times ten thousand great names in its favor do not add a feather's weight to its authority; nor is his confidence in the least shaken if every great man on earth should oppose it. It is a grand thing to be built on the Rock.

The Revelation of Jesus Christ

Note that it is not simply a revelation from Jesus Christ, but the "revelation of Jesus Christ." It was not simply that Christ told Paul something, but that Christ Himself revealed Himself to Paul, and in him, and He is the truth. That this is what is meant here may be seen from verse 16, where we read that God revealed His Son in Paul, that he might preach Him among the heathen. The mystery of the Gospel is Christ in the believer, the hope of glory. Col. 1:25–27. The Holy Spirit is Christ's personal representative. Christ sends Him, that He may abide with us forever. The world receives Him not, because it sees Him not; "but ye know Him," says Christ; "for He {35} dwelleth with you, and shall be in you." John 14:16,17. Only so can the truth of God be known and be made known. Christ does not stand afar off and lay down right principles for us to follow; but He impresses Himself upon us, takes possession of us, as we yield to Him, and makes manifest His life in our mortal flesh. 2 Cor. 4:11. Without this life shining forth, there can be no preaching of the Gospel.

Note that Jesus was revealed in Paul, in order that Paul might preach Him among the heathen. He was not to preach about Christ, but to preach, to present, Christ Himself. "We preach not ourselves, but Christ Jesus the Lord." 2 Cor. 4:5.

God is waiting and anxious to reveal Christ in every man. We read of men "who hold down the truth in unrighteousness," and that "that which may be known of God is manifest in them," even as in everything that God has made His "everlasting power and Divinity" are clearly seen. Rom. 1:18–20, R.V. Now Christ is the truth (John 14:6), and He is the power of God (1 Cor. 1:24), and the Divinity of God (John 1:1). Therefore, Christ is the truth that the wicked are holding down. He is the Divine Word of God, present in men, that they may do it. Deut. 30:14; Rom. 10:6–8. That Christ is in all men is evident from the fact that they live; but He is so held back and kept down that it is difficult to discern Him. Nay, in most men the opposite character is revealed, the mere fact of living and breathing being in many cases the only evidence that Christ is there. Yet He is there, patiently waiting to be revealed,—longing for the time to come when the {36} Word of God may have free course and be glorified, and the perfect life of Jesus of Nazareth be manifested in mortal flesh. This may take place in "whosoever will," no matter how sinful and degraded he is now. It pleases God to do it now; cease, then, to resist.

Personal History

From the twelfth verse of the first chapter till the middle of the second, we have a narrative of personal history, told for a definite purpose. In Paul's experience we see the truth of the Gospel, and how it has nothing to gain from men, but everything to give. The apostle shows that all his early life was against his being influenced by the Gospel, for he studied that which was opposed to it, and he bitterly opposed it. Then he was converted when there was no Christian near him, and he had next to no association with Christians for years afterward. All this of which the Galatians had been previously informed, it was necessary to repeat in order that it might be clear to all that Paul was not bringing them another human invention.

Note, in passing, the word "conversation," which occurs several times in the Bible in a sense that is not now common. Compare the Revised Version, and we find that it means "manner of life." Paul's "conversation in time past" was his early life. See the old and the Revised Version of 1 Pet. 1:18.

"Concerning Zeal, Persecuting the Church"

This is what Paul said of himself, in his Epistle to the Philippians. Phil. 3:6. How great his zeal was he himself tells.

He says that he persecuted the {37} church of God "beyond measure," and "wasted it," or, as in the Revision, "made havoc of it." See also Acts 8:3. Before Agrippa he said: "I verily thought with myself, that I ought to do many things contrary to the name of Jesus of Nazareth. Which thing I also did in Jerusalem; and many of the saints did I shut up in prison, having received authority from the chief priests; and when they were put to death, I gave my voice against them. And I punished them oft in every synagogue, and compelled them to blaspheme; and being exceedingly mad against them, I persecuted them even unto strange cities." Acts 26:9–11. In an address to the Jews in Jerusalem, who knew his life, he said, "I persecuted this way unto the death, binding and delivering into prisons both men and women." Acts 22:4. This he did because, as the previous verse says, he was "zealous toward God." So full of this sort of zeal was he that he breathed nothing but "threatenings and slaughter." Acts 9:1.

It seems almost incredible that any one professing to worship the true God, can have such false ideas of Him as to suppose that He is pleased with that kind of service; yet Saul of Tarsus, one of the most bitter and relentless persecutors of Christians that ever lived, could say years afterward, "I have lived in all good conscience before God until this day." Acts 23:1. Although kicking against the pricks (Acts 9:5), and endeavoring to silence the growing conviction that would force itself upon him as he witnessed the patience of the Christians, and heard their dying testimonies to the truth, Saul was not willfully stifling the voice of conscience. On the contrary, he was {38} striving to preserve a good conscience, and so deeply had he been indoctrinated with the Pharisaic traditions, that he felt sure that these inconvenient prickings must be the suggestions of an evil spirit, which he was in duty bound to suppress. So the prickings of the Spirit of God had for a time only led him to redouble his zeal against the Christians. Of all persons in the world, Saul, the self-righteous Pharisee, had no bias in favor of Christianity. Yet his misdirected zeal was a "zeal for God," and this fact made him good material for a Christian worker.

Paul's Profiting

Paul "profited," made advancement, "in the Jews' religion," above many of his equals, that is, those of his own age, among his countrymen. He had possessed every advantage that was possible to a Jewish youth. "An Hebrew of the Hebrews" (Phil. 3:5), he was nevertheless a free-born Roman citizen (Acts 22:26–28). Naturally quick and intelligent, he had enjoyed the instruction of Gamaliel, one of the wisest doctors of the law, and had been "taught according to the perfect manner of the law of the fathers." Acts 22:3. After the "straitest sect" among the Jews, he lived a Pharisee, and was "a Pharisee of the Pharisees," so that he was "more exceedingly zealous of the traditions" of the fathers than any others of his class. Grown to manhood, he had become a member of the great council among the Jews,—the Sanhedrim,—as is shown by the fact that he gave his vote (Acts 26:10, R.V.) when Christians were condemned to death. Added to this, he possessed the confidence of the high priest, who readily gave him {39} letters of introduction to the rulers of all the synagogues throughout the land, with authority to seize and bind any whom he found guilty of "heresy." He was, indeed, a rising young man, on whom the rulers of the Jews looked with pride and hope, believing that he would contribute much to the restoration of the Jewish nation and religion to their former greatness. There had been a promising future before Saul, from a worldly point of view; but what things were gain to him, those he counted loss for Christ, for whose sake he suffered the loss of all things. Phil. 3:7,8.

The Traditions of the Fathers, not the Religion of Christ

Paul says, "I advanced in the Jews' religion beyond many of mine own age among my countrymen, being more exceedingly zealous for the traditions of my fathers." It is easy to see that "the Jews' religion" was not the religion of God and Jesus Christ, but was human tradition. People make a great mistake in considering "Judaism" as the religion of the Old Testament. The Old Testament no more teaches Judaism than the New Testament teaches Roman Catholicism. The religion of the Old Testament is the religion of Jesus Christ. It was His Spirit that was in the prophets, moving them to present the same Gospel that the apostles afterwards preached. 1 Pet. 1:10–12. When Paul was "in the Jews' religion" he did not believe the Old Testament, which he read and heard read daily, because he did not understand it; if he had, he would have believed on Christ. "For they that dwell at {40} Jerusalem, and their rulers, because they knew Him not, nor yet the voices of the prophets which are read every Sabbath day, they have fulfilled them in condemning Him." Acts 13:27.

The traditions of the fathers led to transgression of the commandments of God. Matt. 15:3. God said of the Jewish people (as a whole): "This people draweth nigh unto Me with their mouth, and honoreth Me with their lips; but their heart is far from Me. But in vain they do worship Me, teaching for doctrines the commandments of men." Verses 8,9. On the Sabbath days the rulers read in the synagogues from the Scriptures, and for this instruction there was no reproof. Jesus said: "The scribes and the Pharisees sit in Moses' seat; all therefore whatsoever they bid you observe, that observe and do; but do not ye after their works; for they say, and do not." Matt. 23:2,3. Jesus had no word condemnation for Moses and his writings. He said to the Jews, "Had ye believed Moses, ye would have believed Me; for he wrote of Me." John 5:46. Everything, therefore, which the scribes read and commanded from his writings was to be followed; but the example of the readers was to be shunned, for they did not obey the Scriptures. Christ said of them, "They bind heavy burdens and grievous to be borne, and lay them on men's shoulders; but they themselves will not move them with one of their fingers." Matt. 23:4. These were not the commandments of God, for "His commandments are not grievous" (1 John. 5:3); and the burdens were not of Christ, for His burden is light (Matt. 11:30).

We hear much about the "Judaizing teachers," {41} who sought to pervert the Galatians, and we know that they who were teaching "another gospel" were Jews; but we must not fall into the error of supposing that these "Judaizing teachers" were presenting the Bible, or any part of it, to the new converts, or trying to get them to follow the Scriptures written by Moses. Far from it; they were leading them away from the Bible, and substituting for its teaching the commandments of men. This was what roused the spirit of Paul. The "Jews' religion" was an entirely different thing from the religion of God, as taught in the law, the prophets, and the psalms.

"Separated unto the Gospel of God"

These are the words with which Paul described himself in the Epistle to the Romans: "Called to be an apostle, separated unto the Gospel of God." Rom. 1:1. So here he says that God "separated me from my mother's womb, and called me by His grace." Gal. 1:15. That God chose Saul to be an apostle, before Saul himself had any thought that he should ever be even a Christian, is evident from the sacred narrative. On his way to Damascus, whither, "breathing out threatenings and slaughter," he was proceeding with full authority to seize, bind, and drag to prison all Christians, both men and women, Saul was suddenly arrested, not by human hands, but by the overpowering glory of the Lord. Three days afterward the Lord said to Ananias, when sending him to give Saul his sight, "He is a chosen vessel unto Me, to bear My name before the Gentiles." Acts 9:15. God arrested Saul in his mad career of persecution, {42} because He had chosen him to be an apostle. So we see that the pricks against which Saul had been kicking were the strivings of the Spirit to turn him to the work to which he had been called.

But how long before this had Saul been chosen to be the messenger of the Lord?—He himself tells us that he was "separated,"—"set apart,"—from his birth. He is not the first one of whom we read that from birth he was chosen to his life-work. Recall the case of Samson. Judg. 13:2–14. John the Baptist was named, and his character and life-work were described, months before he was born. The Lord said to Jeremiah: "Before I formed thee in the belly I knew thee; and before thou camest forth out of the womb I sanctified thee, and I ordained thee a prophet unto the nations." Jer. 1:5. The heathen king Cyrus was named more than a hundred years before he was born, and his part in the work of God was laid out for him. Is. 44:28; 45:1–4.

These are not isolated cases, but are recorded for the purpose of showing us that God rules in the world. It is as true of all men as it was of the Thessalonians, that "God hath from the beginning chosen" them "to salvation through sanctification of the Spirit and belief of the truth." 2 Thess.. 2:13. It rests with every one to make that calling and election sure. And he who "willeth that all men should be saved, and come to the knowledge of the truth" (1 Tim. 2:3,4, R.V.), has also appointed "to every man his work" (Mark 13:34). He who leaves not Himself without witness even in the inanimate creation (Acts 14:17; Rom. 1:20), would fain have man, His highest {43} earthly creation, willingly give such witness to Him as can be given only by human intelligence. All men are chosen to be witnesses for God, and to each is his labor appointed. All through life the Spirit is striving with every man, to induce him to allow himself to be used for the work to which God has called him. Only the Judgment Day will reveal what wonderful opportunities men have recklessly flung away. Saul, the violent persecutor, became the mighty apostle. Who can imagine how much good might have been done by the men whose great power over their fellows has been exerted only for evil, if they had yielded to the influence of the Spirit? Not every one can be a Paul; but the thought that each one, according to the ability that God has given him, is chosen and called of God to witness for Him, will, when once grasped, give to life a new meaning.

The knowledge of this truth will not only make life more real for us, leading us to seek to know the will of God for us individually, and to submit wholly to Him, that He may use us to do the work for which He has designed us, but it will tend to make us more considerate of others, and not to despise the least.

What a wonderful, a joyous, and yet a solemn thought, as we see men moving about, that to each one of them God has given a work of his own to do. They are all servants of the Most High God, each one assigned to special service. It is a wondrous privilege, and a wondrous responsibility. How few are doing the work God would have them do! We should be extremely careful not to hinder any person in the slightest degree from doing his heaven-appointed task. {44}

Another thing that we should remember is that it is God who gives to every man his work. Each one is to receive his orders from God, and not from men. Therefore, we should beware of dictating to men concerning their duty. God can make it plain to them, as well as to us; and if they will not hear Him, they will not be likely to hear us, even if we could direct them in the right way. "It is not in man that walketh to direct his steps" (Jer. 10:23), much less to direct the steps of some other man.

Conferring with Flesh and Blood

"Immediately I conferred not with flesh and blood." This statement is made for the purpose of showing that the apostle did not receive the Gospel from any human being. He saw Christ, and accepted Him, then he went to Arabia, and came back to Damascus, and not till three years after his conversion did he go up to Jerusalem, where he stayed only fifteen days, and saw only two of the apostles. Moreover, the brethren were afraid of him, and would not at first believe that he was a disciple; so it is evident that he did not receive the Gospel from any man.

But there is much to learn from Paul's not conferring with flesh and blood. To be sure, he had no need to, since he had the Lord's own word; but such a course as his is by no means common. For instance, a man reads a thing in the Bible, and then must ask some other man's opinion before he dare believe it. If none of his friends believe it, he is fearful of accepting it. If his pastor, or some commentary, explains the text away, then away it goes; flesh {45} and blood gain the day against the Spirit and the Word.

Or, it may be that the commandment is so plain that there is no reasonable excuse for asking anybody what it means. Then the question is, Can I afford to do it? Will it not cost too much sacrifice? The most dangerous flesh and blood that one can confer with is one's own. It is not enough to be independent of others; in matters of truth one needs to be independent of one's self. "Trust in the Lord with all thine heart; and lean not unto thine own understanding." Prov. 3:5. "He that trusteth in his own heart is a fool." Prov. 28:26.

A pope is one who presumes to occupy the place in counsel which rightfully belongs to God alone. The man who makes himself pope, by following his own counsel, is just as bad as the man who dictates to another, and is more likely to be led astray than is the man who follows some pope other than himself. If one is to follow a pope at all, it would be more consistent to accept the pope of Rome, because he has had more experience in popery than any other. But none is necessary, since we have the Word of God. When God speaks, the part of wisdom is to obey at once, without taking counsel even of one's own heart. The Lord's name is "Counselor" (Is. 9:6), and He is "wonderful in counsel." Hear Him! "He will be our Guide forevermore."

"Immediately"

Note that word. Paul did not stop to parley. He lost no time. He thought he was serving God when he was persecuting the church, and the minute {46} he found out his mistake he turned about. When he saw Jesus of Nazareth, he recognized Him as his Lord, and immediately cried out, "Lord, what wilt Thou have me to do?" He was ready to be set to work in the right way, and that immediately. It is an example well worth consideration. Would that everybody might truthfully say, "I made haste, and delayed not to keep Thy commandments." Ps. 119:60. "I will run the way of Thy commandments, when Thou shalt enlarge my heart." Verse 32.

Gentiles—Heathen.

Paul tells us that Christ was revealed in him, that he might preach Him among the heathen. In the Revision we have the word "Gentiles" used instead of "heathen." There is no difference. The two words are used interchangeably in the English Bible, for wherever they occur, they are translated from only one Greek word, or, if it be in the Old Testament, the corresponding Hebrew word. Let us note a few instances.

In 1 Cor. 12:2 we read, "Ye know that ye were Gentiles, carried away unto these dumb idols, even as ye were led." This is from the ordinary word for "heathen," and the text itself shows that Gentiles are idol-worshipers—heathen. Take notice that the Corinthians "were Gentiles;" they ceased to be such on becoming Christians.

Eph. 2:11,12: "Wherefore remember, that ye being in time past Gentiles in the flesh, who are called Uncircumcision by that which is called the Circumcision in the flesh made by hands; that at that time ye were without Christ, being aliens from the commonwealth {47} of Israel, and strangers from the covenants of promise, having no hope, and without God in the world." Surely, to be a Gentile is to be in a most unenviable condition.

We are told that "God at the first did visit the Gentiles, to take out of them a people for His name." Acts 15:14. And James referred to the believers in Antioch and elsewhere as those who "from among the Gentiles are turned to God." God's people are taken out from among the Gentiles, but on being taken out, they cease to be Gentiles. Abraham, the father of Israel, was taken from among the heathen (Josh. 24:2), so that all Israel are taken from among the Gentiles. Thus it is that "all Israel shall be saved" by the coming in of the fullness of the Gentiles. Rom. 11:25,26.

In Ps. 2:1–3 we might lawfully read, "Why do the Gentiles rage, and the people imagine a vain thing? The kings of the earth set themselves, and the rulers take counsel together, against the Lord, and against His anointed [that is, against Christ, for Christ means 'anointed'], saying, Let us break their bands asunder, and cast away their cords from us." How often we see this fulfilled in the cases of individuals, who, with a triumphant air, exclaim: "Show me a place where the Gentiles are commanded to keep the ten commandments!" meaning that they are Gentiles, and thinking thus to cast away from themselves the laws of God. It is no honorable class in which they place themselves.

It is true that the Gentiles are not commanded to keep the commandments, as Gentiles, for that would be impossible; as soon as {48} they accept Christ, and the law of the Spirit of life in Him, they cease to be Gentiles. How solicitous God is to save people from their Gentile state, is shown by His sending the apostle Paul (to say nothing of Christ) to bring them to Himself.

A Prophet to the Gentiles

In this connection it is worth while to note that God was as anxious for the conversion of the Gentiles three thousand years ago as He is to-day. The Gospel was preached to them before the first advent of Christ, as well as it was afterwards. Paul was not the first one who preached to the Gentiles after Christ, although he was sent specially to them. He was known as the apostle to the Gentiles, yet everywhere he went he preached to the Jews first, and as long as they would hear him. So it was before Christ. By many agencies God made Himself known among all nations, yet Jeremiah was specially chosen as the prophet to the Gentiles, or heathen. In Jer. 1:5, "Before thou camest forth out of the womb I sanctified thee, and I ordained thee a prophet unto the nations," the Hebrew word from which the word "nations" is translated is the very same that is regularly

translated "heathen." "Why do the heathen rage?" Ps. 2:1.
"Proclaim ye this among the Gentiles: Prepare war," etc. "As-
semble yourselves, and come, all ye heathen." Joel 3:9–11. The
words "heathen" and "Gentile" in these texts are the same as
the word "nations," in Jer. 1:5. This can be seen by comparing
the old with the Revised Version. So the Lord said to Jeremiah,
"I sanctified thee, and I ordained thee, a prophet unto the
Gentiles." Let no {49} one say that God ever at any time
confined His truth to any one people, whether Jew or Gentile.
"There is no difference between the Jew and the Greek; for the
same Lord over all is rich unto all that call upon Him." Rom.
10:12.

The New Convert Preaching

As soon as Paul was converted, "straightway he preached
Christ in the synagogues." Acts 9:20. Was it not marvelous that
he should at once be able to preach so powerfully?—Indeed it
was, as it is marvelous that any man can preach Christ. That
anybody should be able to preach Christ in very truth, involves
no less a mystery than Christ manifest in the flesh. But do not
let anybody suppose that Paul got his knowledge instantane-
ously, without any study. Remember that he had all his life been
a diligent student of the Scriptures. It was not an uncommon
thing for a rabbi to be able to repeat the greater portion or the
whole of the Hebrew Scriptures from memory, and we may be
sure that Paul, who had made more advancement than any
others of his age, was as familiar with the words of the Bible as
a bright schoolboy is with the multiplication table. But his mind
was blinded by the traditions of the fathers, which had been
drilled into him at the same time.

The blindness which came upon him when the light shone
round him on the way to Damascus, was but a picture of the
blindness of his mind; and the seeming scales that fell from his
eyes when Ananias spoke to him, indicated the shining forth of
the Word within him, and the scattering of the darkness of
tradition. Paul's case was very different {50} from that of a new
convert who has never read or studied the Bible. Such an one
can, indeed, tell what Christ has done for him, and may thereby
do much good; but he needs much study of the Scriptures to
make him able to show men the way of life perfectly, and lead
them in the way of righteousness.

Paul in Arabia

Many have thought that it was while Paul was in Arabia that
he had his wonderful revelations, and was taken up into heaven,
where he heard "unspeakable words which it is not lawful for
a man to utter." This may well be, although it is by no means
probable that his visions of heavenly things were confined to

that time. All his life through the apostle was in close commun-ion with heaven, and we may be sure that "the heavenly vision" was never hidden from his sight. So, also, we may be sure that, since preaching was his life-work, he did not spend all the months he was in Arabia in study and contemplation. He had been so severe a persecutor, and had received so richly of God's grace, that he counted all the time lost in which he could not reveal that grace to others, feeling, "Woe is me, if I preach not the Gospel." He preached in the synagogues in Damascus, as soon as he was converted, before he went into Arabia; so it is but natural to conclude that he preached the Gospel to the Arabs.

He could preach there without the opposition that he always received when among the Jews, and, therefore, his labors would not so much interfere with his meditation on the new worlds that had just opened before him. {51}

The Persecutor Preaching

Wonderful, indeed, it was to hear that "he that once perse-cuted us, now preacheth the faith of which he once made havoc." In view of the case of Saul of Tarsus, let no one look on any opposer of the Gospel as incorrigible. Those who make opposition are to be instructed with meekness, for who knows but that God will give them repentance to the acknowledgment of the truth? One might have said of Paul, He has had the light as clearly as any man can have it. He has had every opportunity; he has not only heard the inspired testimony of Stephen, but he has heard the dying confessions of many martyrs; he is a hardened wretch, from whom it is useless to expect any good. Yet that same Saul became the greatest preacher of the Gospel, even as he had been the most bitter persecutor. Is there a malignant opposer of the truth? Do not strive with him, and do not reproach him. Let him have all the bitterness and strife to himself, while you hold yourself to the Word of God and to prayer. It may not be long till God, who is now blasphemed, will be glorified in him.

Glorifying God

"And they glorified God in me." How different Paul's case was from that of those to whom he said, "The name of God is blasphemed among the Gentiles through you" (Rom. 2:24)! Every one who professes to be a follower of God should be a means of bringing glory to His name, yet many cause it to be blasphemed; and to have the name of God blasphemed through us is as bad as to be ourselves open {52} blasphemers. How can we cause His name to be glorified?—"Let your light so shine before men, that they may see your good works, and glorify your Father which is in heaven." Matt. 5:16.

Recapitulation

Let us now take a brief glance at the chapter as a whole.

The greeting, embracing the first five verses, tells us the name and calling of the writer of the epistle, and his authority. It incidentally notes the fact that Christ is Divine. A benediction is pronounced, from God the Father, and Jesus Christ the Son. Christ gave Himself for our sins,—purchased them,—thus to deliver us from this present evil world. Our sins constitute this present evil world. Our sins belong to Christ, not to us; so by the power of His death and resurrection, in which He gave Himself for our sins, we may be kept from them. It is the will of God to save us, so that there can be no doubt as to our acceptance. To God belongs the glory, because His is the kingdom and the power.

The next two verses show us the condition of the churches in Galatia at the time the epistle was written, and thus make known to us why it was written. They were departing from God, being led astray by some who were perverting the Gospel of Christ, preaching a pretended gospel instead of the one only Gospel, which is the power of God to salvation to every one that believes. The marvel of the thing is the same as that expressed in Jer. 2:12,13: "Be astonished, O ye heavens, at this, and be horribly afraid, be ye very desolate, saith the Lord. For My {53} people have committed two evils: they have forsaken Me the Fountain of living waters, and hewed them out cisterns, broken cisterns, that can hold no water."

Then in the next two verses (8, 9) we find a curse pronounced on any one, even though it were the apostle himself, or an angel from heaven, who should presume to teach any other gospel than that he had preached. This shows the seriousness of the situation. The Galatian brethren were being placed under the curse by the accursed preachers who preached a false gospel.

Following this, in verses 10–12, the apostle shows himself to be the servant of Christ, because he was seeking to please God only, and not men. The preachers who perverted the souls of men, would preach smooth things,—things in harmony with human nature,—to draw away disciples after them; Paul preached only the plain truth of God, which he received not through any man, but direct from heaven.

Lastly we have the beginning of a little narrative of personal experience, which is continued more than half way through the second chapter. In this Paul refers to his life before his conversion, when he persecuted the church; mentions his conversion, which was the revelation of Christ in him; tells why he was called, and how promptly he responded to the call; and lastly shows how he had no opportunity to get the Gospel from apostles and brethren who were believers before him, even if he had wished to, since he had no connection with them for years after his conversion. The force of this will appear more plainly as we proceed. {54}

Life By The Faith Of Christ, The Truth Of The Gospel

THERE are .doubtless many who are reading this little book, not out of curiosity to see what another person thinks about the Epistle to the Galatians, but for help in arriving at an understanding of that much-discussed portion of Scripture. With each one of these I wish to hold a little personal talk before we proceed further with our study. Every portion of Scripture is connected with every other portion; as soon as we learn one thing thoroughly, making it a part of ourselves, it joins us and aids us in the search for more knowledge, just as each morsel of food that we eat and assimilate assists us in our labor for our daily bread. If, therefore, we proceed in the right way with the study of the Epistle to the Galatians, we shall have opened a wide door to the whole Bible.

The way to knowledge is very simple, so simple that many people despise it. It is not, however, to be despised, for, in spite of the oft-repeated statement to the contrary, there is

A Royal Road to Knowledge

and that road is open to all. Here are the directions, laid down by the king who, to the highest degree, proved it to be the right way:—

"My son, if thou wilt receive My words, and hide {55} My commandments with thee; so that thou incline thine ear unto wisdom, and apply thine heart to understanding; yea, if thou criest after knowledge, and liftest up thy voice for understanding; if thou seekest her as silver, and searchest for her as for hid treasures; then shalt thou understand the fear of the Lord, and find the knowledge of God. For the Lord giveth wisdom; out of His mouth cometh knowledge and understanding." Prov. 2:1–6.

It was in a dream that God appeared to Solomon, and promised to give him wisdom, but it was not by idle dreaming that the wisdom came. Solomon did not go to sleep, and wake up to find himself the wisest man that ever lived. He longed for knowledge so much that he did, indeed, dream of it by night, but he worked for it by day. The foregoing Scripture tells his experience.

Wisdom and knowledge concerning everything are to be found in God's Word; and if you would understand the Word of

God, you must study it. No man on earth can give you his knowledge. Another may aid you by his experience, so that it need not take you as long as it took him; he may direct you how and where to work; but whatever any one really knows he must acquire for himself. When you have traveled over a road a thousand times, you know every turn in it, no matter how many there are, and can see the whole way in your mind. So after you have thought through a portion of Scripture time after time, you will at last be able to see the whole of it, and every separate statement in it, at a single glance. And when you can do that, you will see in it what no man on earth can tell you. {56}

It is useless to think to understand a detached sentence that may present special difficulty, without reference to the connection. If I should bring you a letter, and, pointing to a sentence near the close, should ask you to tell me what my correspondent means, you would at once ask, "What is he writing about? what does he say in what precedes?" If I should reply that I didn't wish you to know the subject of the letter, and would not allow you to read it from the beginning, you would say, "Then I can not help you." But if I should put the letter into your hands, asking you to help me to understand the difficult sentence, you would at once read the letter carefully from the beginning, making sure that you understood everything as you read, and then, with all that preceded the difficult sentence clearly in your mind, you would expect to understand the sentence itself. Even thus reasonably should we deal with the Bible.

Therefore, to each one I say: Study the very words of the text. Go over them again and again; and every time you begin the study of a new portion, go back to the beginning and review all that you have been over. It is a royal method, and it yields royal results.

The first chapter of Galatians gives us a brief, comprehensive view of what the Gospel is, of the condition of the Galatian brethren, and of Paul's personal experience. The second chapter refers to the meeting held in Jerusalem, seventeen years after Paul's conversion, and tells us what was the subject of controversy, and Paul's relation to it. The apostle's sole burden was to preserve "the truth of the Gospel" {57} among the brethren. Having the first chapter clearly in mind, we may proceed to the study of the second, remembering that it is but a continuation of the first.

"Then after the space of fourteen years I went up again to Jerusalem with Barnabas, taking Titus also with me. And I went up by revelation; and I laid before them the Gospel which I preach among the Gentiles, but privately before them who were of repute, lest by any means I should be running, or had run, in vain. But not even Titus who was with me, being a Greek, was compelled to be circumcised; and that because of the false brethren privily brought in, who came in privily to spy out our liberty which we have in Christ Jesus, that they might bring us into bondage; to whom we gave place in the way of subjection, no, not for an hour; that the truth of the Gospel might continue with you. But from those who were reputed to be somewhat (whatsoever they were, it maketh no matter to me: God accepteth no man's person)—they, I say, who were of repute, imparted nothing to me; but contrariwise, when they saw that I had been entrusted with the Gospel of uncircumcision, even as Peter with the Gospel of the circumcision (for He that wrought for Peter unto the apostleship of the circumcision wrought for me also unto the Gentiles); and when they perceived the grace that was given unto me, James and Cephas and John, they who were reputed to be pillars, gave to me and Barnabas the right hands of fellowship, that we should go unto the Gentiles, and they unto the circumcision; only they would that we should remember {58} the poor; which very thing I was also zealous to do.

"But when Cephas came to Antioch, I resisted him to the face, because he stood condemned. For before that certain came from James, he did eat with the Gentiles; but when they came, he drew back and separated himself, fearing them that were of the circumcision. And the rest of the Jews dissembled likewise with him; insomuch that even Barnabas was carried away with their dissimulation. But when I saw that they walked not uprightly according to the truth of the Gospel, I said unto Cephas before them all, If thou, being a Jew, livest as do the Gentiles, and not as do the Jews, how compellest thou the Gentiles to live as do the Jews? We being Jews by nature, and not sinners of the Gentiles, yet knowing that a man is not justified by the works of the law, save through faith in Jesus Christ, even we believed on Christ Jesus, that we might be justified by faith in Christ, and not by the works of the law; because by the works of the law shall no flesh be justified. But if, while we sought to be justified in Christ, we ourselves also were found sinners, is Christ a minister of sin? God forbid. For if I build up again those things which I destroyed, I prove myself a transgressor. For I through the law died unto the law, that I might live unto God. I have been crucified with Christ; yet I live; and yet no longer I, but Christ liveth in me; and that life which I now live in the flesh I live in faith, the faith which is in the Son of God, who loved me, and gave Himself up for me. I do not make void the grace of God; for if righteousness is through the law, then Christ died for naught." Galatians 2, R.V. {59}

Another Visit to Jerusalem

"Fourteen years after," following the natural course of the narrative, means fourteen years after the visit recorded in Gal. 1:18, which was three years after the apostle Paul's conversion. The second visit, therefore, was seventeen years after his conversion, or about the year 51 A.D., which coincides with the time of the conference in Jerusalem, which is recorded in Acts 15. It is with that conference, and the things that led to it, and grew out of it, that the second chapter of Galatians deals. In reading this chapter, therefore, the fifteenth of Acts must be understood and borne in mind.

The New Gospel

In the first chapter of Galatians (verses 6,7) we are told that some were troubling the brethren, by perverting the Gospel of Christ, presenting a false gospel, and pretending that it was the true Gospel. In Acts 15:1 we read that "certain men which came down from Judea taught the brethren, and said, Except ye be circumcised after the manner of Moses, ye can not be saved." This, we see, was the other gospel, which was not another, since there is only one, but which was being palmed off upon the brethren as the true Gospel. That these men who brought this teaching professed to be preaching the Gospel, is evident from the fact that they professed to tell the people what they must do to be saved. Paul and Barnabas would not give any place to the new preaching, but withstood it, in order, as Paul tells the Galatians, "that the truth of the Gospel might continue with you." {60}

Gal. 2:5. The apostles had "no small dissension and disputation with them." Acts 15:2. The controversy was no insignificant one, but was between the real Gospel and a counterfeit. The question was a vital one for the new believers, and has no less interest for us; it concerns our salvation.

A Denial of Christ

A glance at the experience of the church at Antioch, to whom this new gospel was brought, will show that it did in the most direct manner deny the power of Christ to save. The Gospel was first brought to them by brethren who had been scattered by the persecution that arose on the death of Stephen. These brethren came to Antioch "preaching the Lord Jesus. And the hand of the Lord was with them; and a great number believed, and turned unto the Lord." Acts 11:19–21. Then the apostles sent Barnabas to assist in the work; and he, "when he came, and had seen the grace of God, was glad, and exhorted them all, that with purpose of heart they would cleave unto the Lord. For he was a good man, and full of the Holy Ghost and of faith;

and much people was added unto the Lord." Verses 22–24. Then Barnabas found Saul, and together they labored with the church in Antioch for more than a year. Verses 25,26. There were in the church prophets and teachers, and as they ministered unto the Lord, and fasted, the Holy Ghost spoke to them, telling them to separate Barnabas and Saul to the work to which He had called them. Acts 13:1–3. So we see that the church there had had much experience in the things of God. They {61} were acquainted with the Lord and with the voice of the Holy Spirit, who witnessed that they were children of God. And now after all this, these men said to them, "Except ye be circumcised after the manner of Moses, ye can not be saved." That was as much as to say, All your faith in Christ, and all the witness of the Spirit, are nothing without the sign of circumcision. The sign of circumcision, without faith, was exalted above faith in Christ without any outward sign. The new gospel was a most direct assault upon the Gospel, and a flat denial of Christ.

"False Brethren"

It is no wonder that Paul styles those who presented this teaching, "false brethren," who had, as the Danish strongly expresses it, "sneaked in." Gal. 2:4. To the Galatians he said of them, "There be some that trouble you, and would pervert the Gospel of Christ." Gal. 1:7. The apostles and elders, in their letter to the churches, said of those men, "Certain which went out from us have troubled you with words, subverting your souls." Acts 15:24. And they further added that they "gave no commandment" to them. Verse 24, R.V. That is to say, these teachers were "false brethren," who were not recognized by the apostles as teachers, who were speaking perverse things to draw away disciples after themselves. There have been many such since that time. So vicious was their work that the apostle said, "Let them be accursed." They were deliberately seeking to undermine the Gospel of Christ, and thus to destroy the souls of the believers. {62}

"The Sign of Circumcision"

These false brethren had said, "Except ye be circumcised after the manner of Moses, ye can not be saved." Literally, you have not power to be saved. They made salvation only a human thing, resulting solely from the exercise of human power. They had no knowledge of what circumcision really is. "He is not a Jew, which is one outwardly; neither is that circumcision, which is outward in the flesh; but he is a Jew, which is one inwardly; and circumcision is that of the heart, in the Spirit, and not in the letter; whose praise is not of men, but of God." Rom. 2:28,29. There was a time, after Abraham believed God, when he listened to the voice of Sarai, instead of to God, and sought to fulfill the promises of God by the power of his own flesh. See Genesis 16. The result was a failure—a bond-servant instead of an heir. Then God appeared to him again, exhorting him to walk before Him with singleness of heart, and repeating His covenant. As a reminder of his failure, and of the fact that "the flesh profiteth nothing," Abraham received "the sign of circumcision,"—a cutting off of the flesh. This was to show that since in the flesh "dwelleth no good thing," the promises of God can be realized only by the putting off of the body of the sins of the flesh, through the Spirit. "For we are the circumcision, which worship God in the Spirit, and rejoice in Christ Jesus, and have no confidence in the flesh." Phil. 3:3. Abraham was, therefore, really circumcised as soon as he received the Spirit through faith in God. "And he received the sign of {63} circumcision, a seal of the righteousness of the faith which he had yet being uncircumcised." Rom. 4:11. Outward circumcision was never anything more than a sign of the real circumcision of the heart; when this was absent, the sign was a fraud; but when the real circumcision was present, the sign could be dispensed with. Abraham is "the father of all them that believe, though they be not circumcised." The "false brethren" who visited the church at Antioch, subverting the souls of the disciples, and those of the same class who afterwards troubled the Galatians, perverting the Gospel of Christ, were substituting the empty sign for the reality. With them the shell of the nut without the kernel counted for more than the kernel without the shell.

"The Flesh Profiteth Nothing"

Jesus said, "It is the Spirit that quickeneth; the flesh profiteth nothing; the words that I speak unto you, they are Spirit, and they are life." John 6:63. The people of Antioch and Galatia had trusted in Christ for salvation; now there were some who sought to induce them to trust in the flesh. They did not tell them that they were at liberty to sin. Oh, no; they told them that they must keep the law! Yes, they must do it themselves; they must make themselves righteous without Jesus Christ. For circumcision stood for the keeping of the law. Now the real circumcision was the law written in the heart by the Spirit; but these "false brethren" wished the believers to trust in the outward form of circumcision, as a substitute for the Spirit's work; so that the thing which was given as a sign of righteousness {64} by faith, became only a sign of self-righteousness.

The false brethren would have them circumcised for righteousness and salvation; but Peter said, "Through the grace of our Lord Jesus Christ we believe to be saved." Just as Paul wrote, "With the heart man believeth unto righteousness; and with the mouth confession is made unto salvation." Rom. 10:10. "Whatsoever is not of faith is sin." Rom. 14:23. Therefore, all the efforts of men to keep the law of God by their own power, no matter how earnest and sincere they may be, can never result in anything but imperfection—sin. "All our righteousnesses are as filthy rags." Is. 64:6.

"A Yoke of Bondage"

When the question came up in Jerusalem, Peter said to those who would have men seek to be justified by their own works, instead of by faith in Christ, "Now therefore why tempt ye God, to put a yoke upon the neck of the disciples, which neither our fathers nor we were able to bear?" Acts 15:10. This yoke was a yoke of bondage, as is shown by Paul's words, that the "false brethren" sneaked in "to spy out our liberty which we have in Christ Jesus, that they might bring us into bondage." Gal. 2:4. Christ gives freedom from sin. His life is "the perfect law of liberty." "By the law is the knowledge of sin" (Rom. 3:20), but not freedom from it. "The law is holy, and the commandment holy, and just, and good" (Rom. 7:12), just because it gives the knowledge of sin by condemning it. It is a signpost, which points out the way, but does not carry us. It can tell us that we are out of the way; but {65} Jesus Christ alone can make us walk in it; for He is the way. Sin is bondage. Prov. 5:22. Only those who keep the commandments of God are at liberty (Ps. 119:45); and the commandments can be kept only by faith in Christ (Rom. 8:3,4). Therefore, whoever induces people to trust in the law for righteousness, without Christ, simply puts a yoke upon them, and fastens them in bondage. When a man has been convicted by the law as a transgressor, and cast into prison, he can not be delivered from his chains by the law which holds him there. But that is no fault of the law: just because it is a good law, it can not say that a guilty man is innocent. So these Galatian brethren were brought into bondage by men who were foolishly and vainly seeking to exalt the law of God by denying Him who gave it, and in whom alone its righteousness is found.

Why Paul Went Up to Jerusalem

The record in Acts says that it was determined at Antioch that Paul and Barnabas and some others should go up to Jerusalem about this matter. But Paul declares that he went up "by revelation." Gal. 2:2. Paul did not go up simply on their recommendation, but the same Spirit moved both him and them. He did not go up to learn the truth of the Gospel, but to maintain it. He went, not to find out what the Gospel really is, but to communicate the Gospel which he had preached among the heathen. Those who were chief in the conference imparted nothing to him. He had not been preaching for seventeen years that of which he stood in doubt. He knew whom he believed. He {66} had not received the Gospel from any man, and he did not need to have any man's testimony that it was genuine. When God has spoken, an endorsement by man is an impertinence. The Lord knew that the brethren in Jerusalem needed his testimony, and the new converts needed to know that those whom God sent spoke the words of God, and, therefore, all spoke the same thing. They needed the assurance that as they had turned from many gods to the one God, the truth is one, and there is but one Gospel for all men.

The Gospel Not Magic

The great lesson taught by this experience, to which Paul referred the Galatians, is that there is nothing in this world that can confer grace and righteousness upon men, and that there is nothing in the world that any man can do, that will bring salvation. The Gospel is the power of God unto salvation, and not the power of man. Any teaching that leads men to trust in any object, whether it be an image, a picture, or anything else, or to trust for salvation in any work or effort of their own, even though that effort be directed toward the most praiseworthy object, is a perversion of the truth of the Gospel,—a false gospel. There are in the church of Christ no "sacraments" that by some sort of magical working confer special grace on the receiver; but there are things that a man who believes in the Lord Jesus Christ, and who is thereby justified and saved, may do as an expression of his faith. The only thing in the world that has any efficacy in the way of salvation, is the life of God in Christ. "By grace are ye saved through {67} faith; and that not of yourselves; it is the gift of God; not of works, lest any man should boast. For we are His workmanship, created in Christ Jesus unto good works, which God hath before prepared that we should walk in them." Eph. 2:8–10, margin. This is "the truth of the Gospel," and it was for this that Paul stood. It is the Gospel for all time.

Galatians and the Gospel

In this chapter the apostle says that he withstood the false teaching which was now misleading the Galatian brethren, in order that "the truth of the Gospel" might remain with them. Compare this with his introduction, in the first chapter, and his vehement assertions concerning the Gospel which he had preached to them, and his astonishment that they were now forsaking it, and it will be self-evident that the epistle must contain nothing else but the Gospel in the most forcible form of expression. Many have misunderstood it, and have derived no personal gain from it, because they have thought that it was but a contribution to the "strivings about the law," against which Paul himself warned the brethren.

No Monopoly of Truth

"Whatsoever they were, it maketh no matter to me; God accepteth no man's person." There is no man or body of men on earth, that has a monopoly of truth,—a corner, so to speak, so that whoever wishes it must come to him. Truth is independent of men. Truth is of God, for Christ, who is the shining of His glory, and the very impress of His substance (Heb. 1:3), is the truth (John 14:6). {68}

Whoever gets the truth, must get it from God, and not from any man, just as Paul received the Gospel. God may and does use men as instruments, or channels, but He alone is the Giver. Neither names nor numbers have anything to do with determining what is truth. The truth is no more mighty, nor to be accepted more readily, when it is presented by ten thousand princes than when maintained by a single humble, laboring man. And there is no more presumptive evidence that ten thousand men have the truth than that one has it. Every man on earth may be the possessor of just as much of the truth as he is willing to use, and no more. See John 7:17; 12:35,36. He who would act the pope, thinking to hold a monopoly of the truth, and compel people to come to him for it, dealing it out here, and withholding it there, loses all the truth that he ever had, if he ever really had any. Truth and popery can not exist together; no pope, or man with a popish disposition, has the truth. As soon as a man receives the truth, he ceases to be a pope. If the pope of Rome should get converted, and become a disciple of Christ, that very hour he would vacate the papal seat.

The Biggest Not Always the Best

Just as there is no man who has a monopoly of truth, so there are no places to which men must necessarily go in order to find it. The brethren in Antioch did not need to go to Jerusalem to learn the truth, or to find out if what they had was the genuine article. The fact that truth was first proclaimed in a certain place, does not prove that it can be found only there, or that it can be found there {69} at all. In fact, the last places in the world to go to with the expectation of finding or learning truth, are the cities where the Gospel was preached in the first centuries after Christ, as Jerusalem, Antioch, Rome, Alexandria, etc. Paul did not go up to Jerusalem to them that were apostles before him, but began at once to preach.

The Papacy arose in part in this way: It was assumed that the places where the apostles, or some of them, had preached must have the truth in its purity, and that all men must take it from there. It was also assumed that the people of a city must know more of it than the people in the country or in a village. So, from all bishops being on an equality, as at the beginning, it soon came to pass that the "country bishops" (chorepiscopoi) were rated as secondary to those who officiated in the cities. Then, when that spirit crept in, of course the next step was necessarily a strife among the city bishops to see which one should be greatest; and the unholy struggle went on until Rome gained the coveted place of power.

But Jesus was born in Bethlehem, a place that was "little among the thousands of Judah" (Mic. 5:2), and nearly all His life He lived in Nazareth, a little town of so poor repute that a man in whom there was no guile said, "Can there any good thing come out of Nazareth?" John 1:45–47. Afterward Jesus took up His abode in the wealthy city of Capernaum, but was always known as "Jesus of Nazareth." It is no farther to heaven from the smallest village or even the smallest lonely cabin on the plain, than it is from the largest city, or bishop's palace. And God, "the {70} high and lofty One that inhabiteth eternity, whose name is Holy," dwells with him that is of a contrite and humble spirit. Is. 57:15.

Appearances Are Nothing

God looks at what a man is, and not at what he seems to be. What he seems to be is what men estimate him to be, and depends largely on the eyes of those who look at him; what he is, is the measure of the power and wisdom of God that is in him. God does not set any store upon official position. It is not position that gives authority, but authority that gives the real position.

Many a humble, poor man on earth, with never an official title to his name, has occupied a position really higher and of greater authority than that of all the kings of the earth. Authority is the unfettered presence of God in the soul.

It Is God That Works

"He that wrought effectually in Peter to the apostleship of the circumcision, the same was mighty in me toward the Gentiles." The Word of God is living and active. Heb. 4:12, R.V. Whatever activity there is in the work of the Gospel, if there is any work done, is all of God. Jesus "went about doing good," "for God was with Him." Acts 10:38. He Himself said, "I can of Mine own self do nothing." John 5:30. "The Father that dwelleth in Me, He doeth the works." John 14:10. So Peter spoke of Him as "a Man approved of God" "by miracles and wonders and signs, which God did by Him." Acts 2:22. The disciple is not greater than his Lord. {71}

Paul and Barnabas, therefore, at the meeting in Jerusalem, told "what miracles and wonders God had wrought among the Gentiles by them." Acts 15:12. Paul declared that he labored to "present every man perfect in Christ Jesus," "striving according to His working, which worketh in me mightily." Col. 1:28,29. This same power it is the privilege of the humblest believer to possess, "for it is God which worketh in you both to will and to do of His good pleasure." Phil. 2:13. The name of Jesus is Emmanuel, "God with us." God with Jesus caused Him to go about doing good. He is unchangeable; therefore, if we truly have Jesus, God with us, we, likewise, shall go about doing good.

Recognizing the Gift

The brethren in Jerusalem showed their connection with God by recognizing the grace that was given to Paul and Barnabas. When Barnabas first went to Antioch, and saw the grace of God that was working there, he was glad, "and exhorted them all, that with purpose of heart they would cleave unto the Lord. For he was a good man, and full of the Holy Ghost." Acts 11:21–24. Those who are moved by the Spirit of God will always be quick to discern the workings of the Spirit in others. The surest evidence that any one knows nothing personally of the Spirit is that he can not recognize His working. The other apostles had the Holy Spirit, and they perceived that God had chosen Paul for a special work among the Gentiles; and, although his manner of working was different from theirs, for God had given him special gifts for his special work, they freely gave to him {72} the right hand of fellowship, only requesting that he would remember the poor among his own nation; and this he had already shown his willingness to do. Acts 11:27–30. So Paul and Barnabas returned to their work in Antioch.

Perfect Unity

We must not lose sight of the object Paul had in mind in referring to the meeting in Jerusalem. It was to show that there was no difference of opinion among the apostles nor in the church as to what the Gospel is. There were "false brethren," it is true, but inasmuch as they were false, they were no part of the church, the body of Christ, who is the truth. Many professed Christians, sincere persons, suppose that it is almost a matter of necessity that there be differences in the church. "All can not see alike," is the common statement. So they misread Eph. 4:13, making it read that God has given us gifts, "till we all come into the unity of the faith." What the Word teaches is that "in the unity of the faith, and of the knowledge of the Son of God," we all come "unto a perfect man, unto the measure of the stature of the fullness of Christ." There is only "one faith" (Eph. 4:5), "the faith of Jesus," as there is only one Lord; and those who have not that faith must necessarily be out of Christ. It is not at all necessary that there be the slightest difference upon any question of truth. Truth is the Word of God, and the Word of

God is light; nobody but a blind man ever has any trouble to see a light that shines. The fact that a man has never in his life seen any other light used at night, except that from a tallow candle, does not in the least {73} stand in the way of his recognizing that the light from an electric lamp is light, the first moment he sees it. There are, of course, different degrees of knowledge, but never any controversy between those different degrees. All truth is one.

Withstanding Peter

"But when Peter was come to Antioch, I withstood him to the face, because he was to be blamed." We need not magnify nor dwell upon the mistakes of Peter or any other good man, because that is not profitable for us; but we must note this overwhelming proof that Peter was never considered the "prince of the apostles," and that he never was, and never considered himself to be, pope. Fancy any priest, bishop, or cardinal, withstanding Leo XIII. to the face in a public assembly. He would be considered extremely fortunate if the papal guards allowed him to escape with his life for thus presuming to oppose the self-styled "vicar of the Son of God." But Peter made a mistake, and that upon a vital matter of doctrine, because he was not infallible, and he meekly accepted the rebuke that Paul gave him, like the sincere, humble Christian that he was. If there were such a thing as a human head to the church, it would evidently be Paul, instead of Peter, as appears from the whole narrative. Paul was sent to the Gentiles, and Peter to the Jews; but the Jews formed only a very small portion of the church; the converts from the Gentiles soon outnumbered them, so that their presence was scarcely discernible. All these Christians were largely the fruit of Paul's labors, and they naturally looked up to him more than to {74} others, so that Paul could say that upon him daily came "the care of all the churches." 2 Cor. 11:28. But infallibility is not the portion of any man, and Paul himself did not claim it. The greatest man in the church of Christ has no lordship over the weakest. "One is your Master, even Christ; and all ye are brethren." "Be subject one to another."

Making a Difference

When Peter was at the conference in Jerusalem, he told the facts about the receiving of the Gospel by the Gentiles, through his preaching, saying, "God, which knoweth the hearts, bare them witness, giving them the Holy Ghost, even as He did unto us; and put no difference between us and them, purifying their hearts by faith." Acts 15:8,9. God put no difference between Jews and Gentiles in the matter of the purification of the heart, because, knowing the hearts, He knew that "there is no differ-

ence; for all have sinned, and come short of the glory of God,"
so that there is no other way than for all to be "justified freely
by His grace through the redemption that is in Christ Jesus."
Rom. 3:22–24. Yet, after having been shown this fact by the
Lord; after having preached to the Gentiles, and after having
witnessed the gift of the Holy Ghost to them, the same as to
Jewish believers; after having eaten with those Gentile converts,
and faithfully defending his course; after having given a clear
testimony in conference, that God made no difference between
Jews and Gentiles; and even immediately after himself making
no difference, Peter suddenly, as soon as some came who he
thought would not approve of {75} such freedom, began to
make a difference. "He withdrew and separated himself, fearing
them which were of the circumcision." This was, as Paul says,
dissimulation, and was not only wrong in itself, but was calculated to confuse and mislead the disciples. The fact that this was
dissimulation, which was apparent, only emphasizes the fact
that there was no real difference among the brethren. It was
fear, not faith, that for the moment controlled Peter.

Contrary to the Truth of the Gospel

A wave of fear seems to have passed over the Jewish believers,
for "the other Jews dissembled likewise with him; insomuch
that Barnabas also was carried away with their dissimulation."
This in itself was, of course, not walking "uprightly, according
to the truth of the Gospel;" but the mere fact of dissembling was
not the whole of the offense against the truth of the Gospel.
Under the circumstances it was a public denial of Christ, just
as much as that of which Peter had once before, through sudden
fear, been guilty. We have all been too often guilty of the same
sin to permit us to sit in judgment; we can only note the fact
and the natural consequence, as a warning to ourselves.

See how the action of Peter and the others was a virtual,
although unintentional, denial of Christ. There had just been a
great controversy over the question of circumcision. It was a
question of justification and salvation,—whether men were
saved by faith alone in Christ, or by outward forms. Clear
testimony had been borne that salvation is by faith alone: and
now, while the controversy is still alive, {76} while the "false
brethren" are still propagating their errors, these loyal brethren
suddenly discriminated against the Gentile believers, because
they were uncircumcised, in effect saying to them, Except ye be
circumcised, ye can not be saved. Their actions said, We also
are in doubt about the power of faith in Christ alone to save
men; we really believe that salvation depends on circumcision
and the works of the law; faith in Christ is well, but there's
something more to do; it is not in itself sufficient. Such a denial

of the truth of the Gospel Paul could not endure, and he at once struck directly at the root of the matter.

"Sinners of the Gentiles," and Sinners of the Jews

Paul said to Peter, "We...are Jews by nature, and not sinners of the Gentiles." Did he mean that they, being Jews, were, therefore, not sinners?—By no means, for he immediately adds that they had believed on Jesus Christ for justification. They were sinners of the Jews, and not sinners of the Gentiles; but whatever things they had to boast of as Jews, all had to be counted loss for the sake of Christ. Nothing availed them anything except faith in Christ; and since this was so, it was evident that the Gentile sinners could be saved directly by faith in Christ, without going through the dead forms which had been of no service to the Jews, and which were given largely as the result of their unbelief.

"This is a faithful saying, and worthy of all acceptation, that Christ Jesus came into the world to save sinners." 1 Tim. 1:15. "All have sinned," and stand alike guilty before God; but all, of whatever {77} race or class, can accept this saying, "This Man receiveth sinners, and eateth with them." A circumcised sinner is no better than an uncircumcised one; a sinner who stands as a church-member, is no better than one who is outside. The sinner who has gone through the form of baptism is not better than the sinner who has never made any profession of religion. Sin is sin, and sinners are sinners, whether in the church or out; but, thank God, Christ is the propitiation for our sins, as well as for the sins of the whole world. There is hope for the unfaithful professor of religion, as well as for the sinner who has never named the name of Christ. The same Gospel that is preached to the world, must be preached to the church; for there is only one Gospel. It serves to convert sinners in the world, as well as sinners who stand as church-members, and at the same time it renews those who are really in Christ.

"Justified"

"Knowing that a man is not justified by the works of the law," "we have believed in Jesus Christ, that we might be justified," said the apostle. The meaning of the word "justified" is "made righteous." This is the exact term that appears in other languages, which are not composed of foreign terms. The Latin word for righteousness is justitia. To be just is to be righteous. Then we add the termination fy, from the Latin word, meaning "to make," and we have the exact equivalent of the simpler term, "make righteous." In an accommodated sense we use the term "justified" of a man who has not done wrong in a thing whereof he is accused. But, strictly speaking, {78} such an one needs no justification, since he is already just; his righteous deed justified him. He was justified in his deed. But since all have sinned, there are none just or righteous before God; therefore they need to be justified, or made righteous, which God does. Now the law of God is righteousness. See Rom. 7:12; 9:30,31; Ps. 119:172. Therefore Paul did not disparage the law, although he declared that no man could be made righteous by the law, meaning, of course, the law written on stones or in a book. No; so highly did he appreciate the law, that he believed in Christ for the righteousness which the law demands but can not give. "For what the law could not do, in that it was weak through the flesh, God sending His own Son in the likeness of sinful flesh, and for sin, condemned sin in the flesh; that the righteousness of the law might be fulfilled in us, who walk not after the flesh, but after the Spirit." Rom. 8:3,4. The law, which declares all men to be sinners, could not justify them except by declaring that sin is not sin; and that would not be justification, but a self-contradiction in the law.

The Law Can Not Justify

"By the works of the law shall no flesh be justified." Shall we say, Then we will do away with the law? That is what every confirmed criminal thinks. Persistent law-breakers would gladly do away with the law which declares them guilty and will not say that wrong is right. But the law of God can not be abolished, for it is the statement of the will of God. Rom. 2:18. In very fact it is the life and character of God. "The law is holy, and the {79} commandment holy, and just, and good." Rom. 7:12. We read the written law, and find in it our duty made plain. But we have not done it; therefore we are guilty. "All have sinned, and come short of the glory of God." "There is none that doeth good, no, not one." Rom. 3:23,12. Moreover, there is not one who has strength to do the law, its requirements are so great. Then it is very evident that no one can be justified by the works of the law, and it is equally evident that the fault is not in the law, but in the individual. Let the man get Christ in the heart by faith, and then the righteousness of the law will be there also, for Christ says, "I delight to do Thy will, O My God; yea, Thy law is within My heart." Ps. 40:8. He who would throw away the law because it will not call evil good, would reject God because He "will by no means clear the guilty." Ex. 34:7. But God will remove the guilt, will make the sinners righteous, that is, in harmony with the law, and then the law which before condemned them will witness to their righteousness.

"The Faith of Christ"

Much is lost, in reading the Scriptures, by not noting exactly what they say. Here we have literally, "the faith of Christ," just as in Rev. 14:12 we have "the faith of Jesus." He is the Author and Finisher of faith. Heb. 12:2. God has "dealt to every man the measure of faith" (Rom. 12:3), in giving Christ to every man. "Faith cometh by hearing, and hearing by the Word of God" (Rom. 10:17), and Christ is the Word. All things are of God. It is He who gives repentance and forgiveness of sins. {80}

There is, therefore, no opportunity for any one to plead that his faith is weak. He may not have accepted and made use of the gift, but there is no such thing as "weak faith." A man may be "weak in faith," that is, may be afraid to depend on faith, but faith itself is as strong as the Word of God. There is no faith but the faith of Christ; everything else professing to be faith is a spurious article. Christ alone is righteous; He has overcome the world, and He alone has power to do it; in Him dwelleth all the fullness of God, because the law—God Himself—was in His heart; He alone has kept and can keep the law to perfection; therefore, only by His faith,—living faith, that is, His life in us,—can we be made righteous.

But this is sufficient. He is a "tried Stone." The faith which He gives to us is His own tried and approved faith, and it will not fail us in any contest. We are not exhorted to try to do as well as He did, or to try to exercise as much faith as He had, but simply to take His faith, and let it work by love, and purify the heart. It will do it; take it!

Believing Is Receiving

"As many as received Him, to them gave He power to become the sons of God, even to them that believe on His name." John 1:12. That is, as many as believed on His name received Him. To believe on His name is to believe that He is the Son of God; to believe that He is the Son of God, means to believe that He is come in the flesh, in human flesh, in our flesh, for His name is "God with us;" so to believe on His name means simply to believe that He {81} dwells personally in every man,—in all flesh. We do not make it so by believing it; it is so, whether we believe it or not; we simply accept the fact, which all nature reveals to us.

It follows, then, as a matter of course that, believing in Christ, we are justified by the faith of Christ, since we have Him personally dwelling in us, exercising His own faith. All power in heaven and earth is in His hands, and, recognizing this, we simply allow Him to exercise His own power in His own way. God does "exceedingly abundantly," by "the power that worketh in us."

Christ Not the Minister of Sin

Jesus Christ is "the Holy and Righteous One." Acts 3:14, R.V. "He was manifested to take away our sins; and in Him is no sin."

1 John. 3:5. He not only "did no sin" (1 Pet. 2:22), but He "knew no sin" (2 Cor. 5:21). Therefore, it is impossible that any sin can come from Him. He does not impart sin. In the stream of life that flows from the heart of Christ, through His wounded side, there is no trace of impurity. It is "a pure river of water of life, clear as crystal." He is not the minister of sin, that is, He does not minister sin to anybody. If in any one who has sought—and not only sought, but found—righteousness through Christ, there is afterwards found sin, it is because the person has dammed up the stream, allowing the water to become stagnant. The Word has not been given free course, so that it could be glorified; and where there is no activity, there is death. No one is to blame for this but the person himself. Let no professed {82} Christian take counsel of his own imperfections, and say that it is impossible for a Christian to live a sinless life.

It is impossible for a true Christian, one who has full faith, to live any other kind of life. "How shall we, that are dead to sin, live any longer therein?" Rom. 6:2. "Whosoever is born of God doth not commit sin; for His seed remaineth in him; and he can not sin, because he is born of God." 1 John. 3:9. Therefore "abide in Him."

What Was Destroyed?

"If I build up again those things which I destroyed, I prove myself a transgressor." We ask again, What was destroyed, the building up of which will prove us to be transgressors? Remembering that the apostle is talking of those who have believed in Jesus Christ, that they might be justified by the faith of Christ, we find the answer to the question in Rom. 6:6: "Knowing this, that our old man is crucified with Him, that the body of sin might be destroyed, that henceforth we should not serve sin." Also Col. 2:10,11: "Ye are complete in Him, which is the head of all principality and power; in whom also ye are circumcised with the circumcision made without hands, in putting off the body of the sins of the flesh by the circumcision of Christ." That which is destroyed is the body of sin, and it is destroyed only by this personal presence of the life of Christ. It is destroyed in order that we may be freed from its power, and may no longer need to serve it. It is destroyed for everybody, for Christ in His own flesh has abolished "the enmity," the carnal mind; not His own, for He had none, but ours. Our sins, our {83} weaknesses, were upon Him. For every soul the victory has been gained, and the enemy has been disarmed. We have only to accept the victory which Christ has won. The victory over all sin is already a reality; our faith in it makes it real to us. The loss of faith puts us outside the reality, and the old body of sin looms up again. That which is destroyed by faith is built up again by unbelief. Remember that this destruction of the body of sin, although performed by Christ for all, is, nevertheless, a present, personal matter with each individual.

"Dead to the Law"

Many seem to fancy that "dead to the law" means the same as that the law is dead. Not by any means. The law must be in full force, else no one could be dead by means of it. How does a man become dead to the law?—By receiving its full penalty, which is death. He is dead, but the law which put him to death is still as ready as ever to put to death another criminal. Suppose, now, that the man who was executed for gross crimes should, by some miraculous power, come to life again, would he not still be dead to the law?—Certainly; nothing that he had done could be mentioned to him by the law; but if he should again commit crimes, the law would again execute him, but as another man. We say now that I, through the law, am dead to the law, that I might live unto God. By the body of Christ I am raised from the death which I have suffered by the law because of my sin, and now I walk "in newness of life," a life unto God. Like Saul of old, I am by the Spirit of God "turned into another man." 1 Sam. 10:6. {84}

This is the Christian's experience. That this is the case is shown by what follows.

Crucified with Christ

"I am crucified with Christ; nevertheless I live; yet not I, but Christ liveth in me." Christ was crucified; He was "delivered for our offenses, and raised again for our justification." Rom. 4:25. But unless we are crucified with Him, His death and resurrection profit us nothing. If the cross of Christ is separated from us, and outside of us, even though it be but by so much as a moment of time and an hair's breadth of space, it is to us all the same as if He were not crucified. No one was ever saved simply by looking forward to a cross to be erected and a Christ to be crucified at some indefinite time in the future, and no one can now be saved simply by believing that at a certain time in the past Christ was crucified. No; if men would see Christ crucified, they must look neither forward nor backward, but upward; for the arms of the cross that was erected on Calvary reach from Paradise lost to Paradise restored, and embrace the whole world of sin. The crucifixion of Christ is not a thing of but a single day. He is "the Lamb that hath been slain from the foundation of the world" (Rev. 13:8, R.V.); and the pangs of Calvary will not be ended as long as a single sin or sinner exists in the universe. Even now Christ bears the sins of the whole world, for "in Him all things consist;" and when at the last He is obliged to cut off the irreclaimably wicked in the lake of fire, the anguish which they suffer will be {85} only that which the Christ whom they have rejected suffered on the cross.

Where the Cross Is

Christ bore our sins in His own body on the tree. 1 Pet. 2:24. He was "made a curse for us," in that He hung on the tree. Gal. 3:13. On the cross He bore not only the weakness and sin of humanity, but also the weakness of the earth. Thorns are the sign of the curse, the weakened, imperfect condition of the earth (Gen. 3:17,18; 4:11,12); and on the cross Christ bore the crown of thorns. Therefore, all the curse, every trace of it, is borne by Christ,—by Christ crucified. Wherever, therefore, we see any curse, or wherever there is any curse, whether we see it or not, there is the cross of Christ. This can be seen again from the following: The curse is death, and death kills; the curse is in everything, yet everywhere we see life. Here is the miracle of the cross. Christ suffered the curse of death, and yet lived. He is the only one that could do it. Therefore, the fact that we see life everywhere, also in ourselves, in spite of the curse which is everywhere, is positive proof that the cross of the Crucified One is there bearing it. So it is that not only every blade of grass, every leaf of the forest, and every piece of bread that we eat has the stamp of the cross of Christ on it, but, above all, we have the same. Wherever there is a fallen, sin-scarred, miserable human being, there is also the Christ of God crucified for him and in him. Christ on the cross bears all things, and the sins of that man are on Him. Because of unbelief and {86} ignorance the man feels all the weight of the heavy burden, but the load is on Christ, nevertheless. It is easy for Christ, but heavy for the man; if the man will believe, he may be relieved of the load. In short, Christ bears the sins of all the world on the cross. Therefore, wherever sin is found, there we may be sure is the cross of Christ.

Where Sin Is

Sin is a personal matter. A man is guilty only of his own sins, and not of those which another has committed. Now I can not sin where I am not, but only where I am. Sin is in the heart of man; "for from within, out of the heart of men, proceed evil thoughts, adulteries, fornications, murders, thefts, covetousness, wickedness, deceit, lasciviousness, an evil eye, blasphemy, pride, foolishness; all these evil things come from within." Mark 7:21–23. "The heart is deceitful above all things, and desperately wicked." Jer. 17:9. Sin is in every fiber of our being by nature. We are born in sin, and our life is sin, so that sin can not be taken from us without taking our life. What I need is freedom from my own personal sin,—that sin which not only has been committed by me personally, but which dwells in the heart,—the sin which constitutes the whole of my life.

Bound by Sin

"His own iniquities shall take the wicked himself, and he shall be holden with the cords of his sins." Prov. 5:22. "For though thou wash thee with niter, and take thee much soap, yet thine iniquity is marked before Me, saith the Lord." Jer. 2:22. My sin is committed {87} by myself, in myself, and I can not separate it from me. Cast it on the Lord? Ah, yes, that is right, but how? Can I gather it up in my hands, and cast it from me, so that it will light upon Him?—I can not. If I could separate it but a hair's breadth from me, then I should be safe, no matter what became of it, since it would not be found in me. In that case I could dispense with Christ; for if sin were not found on me, it would make no matter to me where it was found. If I could gather up my sins so as to lay them upon Christ crucified apart from me, then I would not need to put them on Him. They would then be away from me, and that would clear me. But no works of any kind that I can do can save me; therefore, all my efforts to separate myself from my sins are unavailing.

Christ Bears the Sin in Us

It is evident from what has been said that whoever bears my sins must come where I am, yea, must come into me. And this is just what Christ does. Christ is the Word, and to all sinners, who would excuse themselves by saying that they can not know what God requires of them, He says, "The Word is very nigh unto thee, in thy mouth, and in thy heart, that thou mayest do it." Deut. 30:11–14. Therefore, He says, "If thou shalt confess with thy mouth the Lord Jesus, and shalt believe in thine heart that God hath raised Him from the dead, thou shalt be saved." Rom. 10:9. What shall we confess about the Lord Jesus?—Why, confess the truth, that He is nigh thee, even in thy mouth and in thy heart, and believe that He is there risen from the dead. "Now {88} that He ascended, what is it but that He also descended first into the lower parts of the earth?" Eph. 4:9. The risen Saviour is the crucified Saviour. As Christ risen is in the heart of the sinner, therefore, Christ crucified is there. If it were not so, there would be no hope for any. A man may believe that Jesus was crucified eighteen hundred years ago, and may die in his sins; but he who believes that Christ is crucified and risen in him, has salvation.

All that any man in the world has to do in order to be saved, is to believe the truth, that is, to recognize and acknowledge facts, to see things just as they actually are, and to confess them. Whoever believes that Christ is crucified in him, which is the fact in the case of every man, and confesses that the crucified

Christ is also risen, and that He dwells in him by and with the power of the resurrection, is saved from sin, and will be saved as long as he holds fast his confession. This is the only true confession of faith.

What a glorious thought that, wherever sin is, there is Christ, the Saviour from sin! He bears sin, all sin, the sin of the world. Sin is in all flesh, and so Christ is come in the flesh. Christ is crucified in every man that lives on earth. This is the word of truth, the Gospel of salvation, which is to be proclaimed to all, and which will save all who accept it.

Living by Faith

In the tenth chapter of Romans, as already noted, we learn that Christ is in every man, "a very present help in trouble." He is in the sinner, in order {89} that the sinner may have every incentive and facility for turning from sin to righteousness. He is "the way, the truth, and the life." n 14:6. There is no other life than His. He is the life. But, although He is in every man, not every man has His righteousness manifested in his life; for some "hold down the truth in unrighteousness." Rom. 1:18, R.V. Now Paul's inspired prayer was that we might be strengthened with might by the Spirit of God in the inner man, "that Christ may dwell in your hearts by faith;" "that ye might be filled with all the fullness of God." Eph. 3:16–19. The difference, then, between the sinner and the Christian is this: that, whereas Christ crucified and risen is in every man, in the sinner He is there unrecognized and ignored, while in the Christian He dwells there by faith.

Christ is crucified in the sinner, for wherever there is sin and the curse, there is Christ bearing it. All that is needed now is for the sinner to be crucified with Christ, to let Christ's death be his own death, in order that the life of Jesus may be manifested in his mortal flesh. Faith in the eternal power and Divinity of God, that are seen in all the things that He has made, will enable any one to grasp this mystery. The seed is not quickened "except it die." 1 Cor. 15:36. "Except a corn of wheat fall into the ground and die, it abideth alone; but if it die, it bright forth much fruit." n 12:24. So the one who is crucified with Christ, begins at once to live, but it is as another man. "I live; yet not I, but Christ liveth in me." {90}

The Life of the World

"But Christ was actually crucified eighteen hundred years, and more, ago, was He not?"—Certainly. "Then how can it be that my personal sins were upon Him? or how can it be that I am now crucified with Him?"—Well, it may be that we can not understand the fact, but that makes no difference with the fact.

But when we remember that Christ is the life, even "that eternal life, which was with the Father, and was manifested unto us" (1 n. 1:2), we may understand something of it. "In Him was life; and the life was the light of men,"—"the true light, which lighteth every man that cometh into the world." n 1:4,9.

Christ is larger than the Man Jesus of Nazareth, whom the eyes of all men could see. Flesh and blood,—that which the eyes can see,—can not reveal "the Christ, the Son of the living God." Matt. 16:16,17. "Eye hath not seen, nor ear heard, neither have entered into the heart of man, the things which God hath prepared for them that love Him. But God hath revealed them unto us by His Spirit." 1 Cor. 2:9,10. So no man, no matter how well acquainted he was with the Carpenter of Nazareth, could call Him Lord but by the Holy Ghost. 1 Cor. 12:3. By the Spirit, His own personal presence, He can dwell in every man on earth, and fill the heavens as well, a thing which Jesus in the flesh could not do. Therefore, it was expedient for Him to go away, and send the Comforter. "He is before all things, and in Him all things consist." Col. 1:16,17, R.V. Jesus of Nazareth was the manifestation of Christ in the flesh; {91} but the flesh was not Christ, for "the flesh profiteth nothing." It is the Word which was in the beginning, and whose power upholds all things, that is the Christ of God. The sacrifice of Christ, so far as this world is concerned, dates from the foundation of the world. While Christ was going about doing good in Judea and Galilee, He was in the bosom of the Father making reconciliation for the sins of the world.

The scene on Calvary was the manifestation of what has taken place as long as sin has existed, and will take place until every man is saved who is willing to be saved: Christ bearing the sins of the world. He bears them now. One act of death and resurrection was sufficient for all time, for it is eternal life that we are considering; therefore, it is not necessary for the sacrifice to be repeated. That life pervades and upholds all things, so that whoever accepts it by faith has all the benefit of the entire sacrifice of Christ. By Himself He "made purification of sins." Whoever rejects the life, or is unwilling to acknowledge that the life which he has is Christ's life, loses, of course, the benefit of the sacrifice.

The Faith of the Son of God

Christ lived by the Father. n 6:57. His faith in the word that God gave Him was such that He repeatedly and positively maintained that when He died He should rise again the third day. In this faith He died, saying, "Father, into Thy hands I commend My Spirit." Luke 23:46. That faith which gave Him the victory over death (Heb. 5:7), because it gave Him the complete victory over sin, {92} is the faith which He exercises in us, when He dwells in us by faith; for He is "the same yesterday, and today, and forever." It is not we that live, but Christ that lives in us, and uses His own faith to deliver us from the power of Satan. "What have we to do?"—Let Him live in us in His own way. "Let this mind be in you, which was also in Christ Jesus." How can we let Him?—Simply by acknowledging Him; by confessing Him. We can not understand, so as to explain the mystery of Christ in us the hope of glory, but everything in nature that serves to sustain our life teaches us the fact. The sunlight that shines upon us, the air that we breathe, the food that we eat, and the water that we drink, are all means of conveying life to us. The life that they convey to us is none other than the life of Christ, for He is the life, and thus we have constantly before us and in us evidence of the fact that Christ can live in us. If we allow the Word to have free course in us, it will be glorified in us, and will glorify us.

The Gift for Me

"Who loved me, and gave Himself for me." How personal this is. I am the one whom He loved. Each soul in the world can say, "He loved me, and gave Himself for me." Leave Paul out of the question in reading this. Paul is dead, but the words that he wrote are yet alive. It was true of Paul, but no more so than of every other man. They are the words which the Spirit puts in our mouths, if we will but receive them. The whole gift of Christ is for each individual me. Christ is not divided, but every soul gets the whole of Him, just the same as if there were not another {93} person in the world. Each one gets all the light that shines. The fact that there are millions of people for the sun to shine upon, does not make its light any the less for me; I get the full benefit of it, and could not get more if I were the only person in the world. It shines for me. So Christ gave Himself for me, the same as if I were the only sinner in the world; and the same is true of every other sinner. When you sow a grain of wheat, you get many more grains of the same kind, each one having the same life, and just as much of it, as the original seed had. So it is with Christ, the true Seed. In dying for us, that we may also become the true seed, He gives to every one of us the whole of His life. "Thanks be unto God for His unspeakable gift."

Christ Not Dead in Vain

"I do not frustrate the grace of God; for if righteousness come by the law, then Christ is dead in vain." This is the summing up of the case. It is the substance of what has preceded. If righteousness came by the law, then there would have been no use for the death of Christ. The law itself can do nothing except point out men's duty; therefore, to speak of righteousness coming by the law, means by our works, by our individual effort. So the text is equivalent to the statement that if we could save ourselves, Christ died for nothing; for salvation is the one thing to be gained. Well, we can not save ourselves; and Christ is not dead in vain; therefore there is salvation in Him. He is able to save all that come unto God by Him. Some must be saved, else He has {94} died in vain; but He has not died in vain; therefore, the promise is sure: "He shall see His seed, He shall prolong His days, and the pleasure of the Lord shall prosper in His hand, He shall see of the travail of His soul, and shall be satisfied." Is. 53:10,11. "Whosoever will," may be of the number. Since He died not in vain, see to it "that ye receive not the grace of God in vain." {95}

Redeemed From The Curse,
To The Blessing Of Abraham

THE two chapters of Galatians that we have already studied give us sufficient idea of the entire book, so that we can practically take leave of the Galatian brethren, and consider it as addressed solely to us. The circumstances that called forth the writing of the epistle were that the Galatians, having accepted the Gospel, were led astray by false teachers, who presented to them "another gospel," that is, a counterfeit gospel, since there is but one for all time and for all men. The way it was presented to them was, "Except ye be circumcised after the manner of Moses, ye can not be saved." Outward circumcision was given as a sign of righteousness which the individual already possessed by faith. Rom. 4:11. It was a sign that the law was written in the heart by the Spirit, and it was, therefore, only a mockery and a sham when the law was transgressed. Rom. 2:25–29. But for one to be circumcised in order to be saved, was to put his trust in works of his own and not in Christ. Now, although there is in these days no question as to whether or not a man should submit to the specific rite of circumcision in order to be saved, the question of salvation itself, whether by human works or by Christ alone, is as live a one as ever. {96}

Instead of attacking their error, and combating it with hard argument, the apostle begins with experience, the relation of which illustrates the case in hand. In this narrative he has occasion to show that salvation is wholly by faith, for all men alike, and not in any degree by works. As Christ tasted death for every man, so every man who is saved must have Christ's personal experience of death and resurrection and life. Christ in the flesh does what the law could not do. Gal. 2:21; Rom. 8:3,4. But that very fact witnesses to the righteousness of the law. If the law were at fault, Christ would not fulfill its demands. He shows its righteousness by fulfilling, or doing, what it demands, not simply for us, but in us. The grace of God in Christ attests the majesty and holiness of the law. We do not frustrate the grace of God; if righteousness could come by the law, then would Christ be dead in vain. But to claim that the law could be abolished, or could relax its claims, and thus be of no account, is also to say that Christ is dead in vain. Let it be repeated, righteousness can not possibly come by the law, but only by the faith of Christ; but the fact that the righteousness of the law could be attained in no other way by us than by the crucifixion and resurrection and life of Christ in us, shows the infinite greatness and holiness of the law.

"O foolish Galatians, who did bewitch you, before whose eyes Jesus Christ was openly set forth crucified? This only would I learn from you, Received ye the Spirit by the works of the law, or by the hearing {97} of faith? Are ye so foolish? having begun in the Spirit, are ye now perfected in the flesh? Did ye suffer so many things in vain? if it be indeed in vain. He therefore that supplieth to you the Spirit, and worketh miracles among you, doeth he it by the works of the law, or by the hearing of faith? Even as Abraham believed God, and it was reckoned unto him for righteousness. Know therefore that they which be of faith, the same are sons of Abraham. And the Scripture, foreseeing that God would justify the Gentiles by faith, preached the Gospel beforehand unto Abraham, saying, In thee shall all the nations be blessed. So then they which be of faith are blessed with the faithful Abraham. For as many as are of the works of the law are under a curse; for it is written, Cursed is every one which continueth not in all things that are written in the book of the law, to do them. Now that no man is justified by the law in the sight of God, is evident; for, The righteous shall live by faith; and the law is not of faith; but, He that doeth them shall live in them. Christ redeemed us from the curse of the law, having become a curse for us; for it is written, Cursed is every one that hangeth on a tree; that upon the Gentiles might come the blessing of Abraham in Christ Jesus; that we might receive the promise of the Spirit through faith.

"Brethren, I speak after the manner of men, Though it be but a man's covenant, yet when it hath been confirmed, no one maketh it void, or addeth thereto. Now to Abraham were the promises spoken, and to his seed. He saith not, And to seeds, {98} as of many; but as of one, And to thy seed, which is Christ. Now this I say: A covenant confirmed beforehand by God, the law, which came four hundred and thirty years after, doth not disannul, so as to make the promise of none effect. For if the inheritance is of the law, it is no more of promise; but God hath granted it to Abraham by promise. What then is the law? It was added because of transgressions, till the seed should come to whom the promise hath been made; and it was ordained through angels by the hand of a mediator. Now a mediator is not a mediator of one; but God is one. Is the law then against the promises of God? God forbid; for if there had been a law given which could make alive, verily righteousness would have been of the law. Howbeit the Scripture hath shut up all things under sin, that the promise by faith in Jesus Christ might be given to them that believe.

"But before faith came, we were kept in ward under the law, shut up unto the faith which should afterwards be revealed. So that the law hath been our tutor to bring us unto Christ, that we might be justified by faith. But now that faith is come, we are no longer under a tutor. For ye are all sons of God, through faith, in Christ Jesus. For as many of you as were baptized into Christ did put on Christ. There can be neither Jew nor Greek, there can be neither bond nor free, there can be no male and female; for ye all are one man in Christ Jesus. And if ye are Christ's, then are ye Abraham's seed, heirs according to promise." Galatians 3, R.V. {99}

The Sin of Witchcraft

The apostle asks those who are departing from God and His truth, "Who hath bewitched you?" "Behold, to obey is better than sacrifice, and to hearken than the fat of rams. For rebellion is as the sin of witchcraft, and stubbornness is as iniquity and idolatry." 1 Sam. 15:22,23. If you look up this text in the Bible, you will see that in both instances the words "is as" are added. The literal Hebrew is, "Rebellion is the sin of witchcraft, and stubbornness is iniquity and idolatry." And how so?—Plainly enough, for stubbornness and rebellion are rejection of God; and he who rejects God, puts himself under the control of evil spirits. All idolatry is devil-worship. "The things which the Gentiles sacrifice, they sacrifice to devils." 1 Cor. 10:20. There is no middle ground. Christ says, "He that is not with Me is against Me." Matt. 12:30. That is, disobedience, rejection of the Lord, is the spirit of antichrist. The Galatian brethren were, as we have already seen, departing from God, and consequently they were inevitably, although perhaps unconsciously, relapsing into idolatry.

The Safeguard against Spiritualism

Spiritualism is only another name for ancient witchcraft and soothsaying. It is a fraud, but not the kind of fraud that most people think it is. There is reality in it. It is a fraud in that while it professes to receive communications from the spirits of the dead, it has communication only with the spirits of devils, since "the dead know {100} not anything." To be a Spiritualist medium is to give one's self to the control of demons. Now there is only one protection against this, and that is to hold fast to the Word of God. He who lightly regards God's Word, severs himself from association with God, and puts himself within Satan's influence. Even though a man denounce Spiritualism in the strongest terms, if he does not hold to God's Word, he will sooner or later be carried away by the strong delusion. Only by keeping the Word of Christ's patience can men be kept from the temptation that is coming on all the world. Rev. 3:10. "The spirit that now worketh in the children of disobedience" (Eph. 2:2), is the spirit of Satan, the spirit of antichrist; and the Gospel of Christ, which reveals the righteousness of God (Rom. 1:16,17), is the only possible salvation from it.

Christ Crucified before Us

"Who did bewitch you, before whose eyes Jesus Christ was openly set forth crucified?" Jesus was set forth before the Galatians, when Paul preached to them, as openly crucified before their eyes. So vivid was the presentation, that they could actually see Christ crucified. It was not skillful word-painting on the part of Paul, nor imagination on the part of the Galatians, for then it would have been only deception. No; it was an actual fact; Christ was there, crucified, before their eyes, and Paul by the Spirit enabled them to see Him. We know that it was not Paul's skill in making beautiful word pictures that enabled them to fancy that they saw the crucifixion, for elsewhere Paul says that he determined {101} to know nothing but Jesus Christ and Him crucified, and that he purposely and carefully refrained from using the wisdom of words, for fear that he should make the cross of Christ without effect. 1 Cor. 1:17,18; 2:1–4. The experience of the Galatians in this matter was not peculiar to them. The cross of Christ is a present thing. The expression, "Come to the cross," is not an empty form of words, but an invitation that can be literally complied with. Christ is crucified before us, and each blade of grass, each leaf in the forest, reveals the fact. Yea, we have the testimony in our own bodies, in that, although sinful and corruptible, we yet live. Not until one has seen Christ crucified before his eyes, and can see the cross of Christ at every turn, does one know the reality of the Gospel. Let those scoff who will; the fact that a blind man can not see the sun, and denies that it shines, will not deter one who sees it from talking of its glory. Many there are who can testify that it is something more than a figure of speech, when the apostle says that Christ was crucified before the eyes of the Galatians. They have had the experience. God grant that this study of Galatians, before it is finished, may be the means of opening the eyes of many more, so that they may see Christ crucified before their eyes, and know Him crucified in them and for them.

A Good Beginning

The question, "Received ye the Spirit by the works of the law, or by the hearing of faith?" admits of but one answer. It was by the hearing of faith. The Spirit is given to those who believe. John 7:39; Eph. 1:13. {102} The question also shows that the Galatians had received the Holy Spirit. There is no other way of beginning the Christian life. "No man can say that Jesus is the Lord, but by the Holy Ghost." 1 Cor. 12:3. In the beginning the Spirit of God moved upon the face of the waters, begetting life and activity in the creation; for without the Spirit there is no motion—no life. "Not by might, nor by power, but by My Spirit, saith the Lord of hosts." Zech. 4:6. The Spirit of God alone can carry out the perfect will of God, and no works that a man can do can bring Him into the soul, any more than a dead man can manufacture the breath by which he can be made to live and move. Those to whom Paul addressed this Epistle had seen Christ crucified before their eyes, and had accepted Him through the Spirit. Have you also seen and accepted Him?

Hold Fast the Beginning

"Are ye so foolish? having begun in the Spirit, are ye now perfected in the flesh?" Foolish is but a feeble term for it. The man who has not power to begin a work, has strength to finish it! He who has not strength to put one foot before the other, or even to stand alone, has strength enough in himself to win a race! Impossible. Who has power to beget himself? No one; we come into this world without having begotten ourselves; we are born without strength; and, therefore, all the strength that ever manifests itself in us, comes from another than ourselves. It is all given to us. The new-born babe is the representative of man. "A man is born into the world." All the strength that any man has {103}of himself is found in the infant as it utters its first cry with its first breath. And even that feeble strength is not of itself. Even so in things spiritual. "Of His own will begat He us with the Word of truth." Jam. 1:18. We can no more live righteous lives by our own strength than we could beget ourselves. The work that is begun by the Spirit, must be carried to completion by the Spirit. "We are made partakers of Christ, if we hold the beginning of our confidence steadfast unto the end." Heb. 3:14. "He which hath begun a good work in you will perform it until the day of Jesus Christ." Phil. 1:6. And He alone can do it.

Experience in the Gospel

"Have ye suffered so many things in vain? if it be yet in vain. He therefore that ministereth to you the Spirit, and worketh miracles among you, doeth he it by the works of the law, or by the hearing of faith?" These questions show that the experience of the Galatian brethren had been as deep and as real as would be expected from those before whose eyes Christ was openly crucified. The Spirit had been given to them, miracles had been wrought among them, and even by them, for the gifts of the Spirit accompany the gift of the Spirit; and as the result of this living Gospel among them, they had suffered persecution; for "all that will live godly in Christ Jesus shall suffer persecution." 2 Tim. 3:12. This makes the case the more serious. Having shared the sufferings of Christ, they were now departing from

Him; and this departure from Christ, through whom alone righteousness can come, was {104} marked by disobedience to the law of truth. They were insensibly but inevitably transgressing the law to which they were looking for salvation.

Abraham Believed God

The questions asked in verses 3, 4, and 5 suggest their own answer. The Spirit was ministered, and miracles were wrought, not by works of law, but by "the hearing of faith," that is, by the obedience of faith, for faith comes by hearing the Word of God. Rom. 10:17. Thus Paul's labor, and the first experience of the Galatians, were exactly in line with the experience of Abraham, whose faith was accounted for righteousness. Let it be remembered that the "false brethren" who preached "another gospel," even the false gospel of righteousness by works, were Jews, and claimed Abraham for their father. It would be their boast that they were children of Abraham, and they would appeal to their circumcision as proof of the fact. But the very thing upon which they relied as proving them to be children of Abraham, was proof that they were not; for "Abraham believed God, and it was accounted to him for righteousness." Abraham had the righteousness of faith before he was circumcised. Rom. 4:11. "Know ye therefore that they which are of faith, the same are the children of Abraham." Abraham was not justified by works (Rom. 4:2,3), but his faith "wrought righteousness."

The same trouble still exists. People take the sign for the substance, the end for the means. They see that righteousness reveals itself in good works; therefore, they assume that the good works bring the {105} righteousness. Righteousness gained by trusting, good works wrought without working, seem to them impractical and fanciful. They call themselves "practical" men, and believe that the only way to have a thing done is to do it. But the truth is that all such men are highly impractical. A man absolutely "without strength" can not do anything, not even so much as raise himself up to take the medicine that is offered him; and any counsel for him to try to do it would be impractical. Only in the Lord is there righteousness and strength. Is. 45:24. "Commit thy way unto the Lord; trust also in Him; and He shall bring it to pass. And He shall bring forth thy righteousness as the light." Ps. 37:5,6. Abraham is the father of all who believe for righteousness, and of those only. The only practical thing is to trust, even as he did.

The Gospel to the Gentiles

"The Scripture, foreseeing that God would justify the Gentiles by faith, preached the Gospel beforehand unto Abraham." This verse will bear much reading. An understanding of it will guard one against many errors. And it is not difficult to understand; simply hold to what it says, and you have it.

(a) For one thing, the verse shows us that the Gospel was preached at least as early as the days of Abraham.

(b) It was God Himself who preached it; therefore, it was the true and only Gospel.

(c) It was the same Gospel that Paul preached; so {106} that we have no other Gospel than that which Abraham had.

(d) The Gospel differs in no particular now from what it was in Abraham's day; for his day was the day of Christ. n 8:56.

God requires just the same things now that He required then, and nothing more.

Moreover, the Gospel was then preached to the Gentiles, for Abraham was a Gentile, or, in other words, a heathen. He was brought up as a heathen, for "Terah, the father of Abraham," "served other gods" (Josh. 24:2), and was a heathen till the Gospel was preached to him. So the preaching of the Gospel to the Gentiles was no new thing in the days of Peter and Paul. The Jewish nation was taken out from among the heathen, and it is only by the preaching of the Gospel to the heathen that Israel is built up and saved. See Acts 15:14–18; Rom. 11:25,26. The very existence of the people Israel always was and still is a standing proof that God's purpose is to save a people from among the Gentiles. It is in fulfillment of this purpose that Israel exists.

Thus we see that the apostle takes the Galatians, and us, back to the fountain-head,—to the place where God Himself preaches the Gospel to us Gentiles. No Gentile can hope to be saved in any other way or by any other gospel than that by which Abraham was saved.

Blessed with Abraham

"So then they which be of faith are blessed with faithful Abraham." Mark the close connection between this and the preceding verse. The Gospel was {107} preached to Abraham in the words, "In thee shall all nations be blessed." (It should be remembered, in passing, that the words "heathen," or "Gentiles," as in the Revised Version, and "nations," in verse 8, come from the very same Greek word.) This blessing is the blessing of righteousness through Christ, as we learn from Acts 3:25,26: "Ye are the children of the prophets, and of the covenant which God made with our fathers, saying unto Abraham, And in thy seed shall all the kindreds of the earth be blessed. Unto you first God, having raised up His Son Jesus, sent Him to bless you, in turning away every one of you from his iniquities." Because God preached the Gospel to Abraham, saying, "In thee shall all the nations of the earth be blessed," those who believe are blessed with the faithful Abraham. There is no blessing for any man except the blessing which Abraham received, and the Gospel preached to him is the only Gospel there is for any people under heaven; for besides the name of Jesus, in whom Abraham believed, "there is none other name under heaven given among men whereby we must be saved." In Him "we have redemption through His blood, even the forgiveness of sins." Col. 1:14. The forgiveness of sins carries with it all blessings.

A Contrast: Under the Curse

Note the sharp contrast in verses 9 and 10. "They which be of faith are blessed," but "as many as are of the works of the law are under the curse." Faith brings the blessing; works bring the curse, or, rather, leave one under the curse. The curse is on all, for "he that believeth not is condemned {108} already, because he hath not believed in the name of the only-begotten Son of God." n 3:18. Faith removes the curse.

Who are under the curse?—"As many as are of the works of the law." Note that it does not say that those who do the law are under the curse, for that would be a contradiction of Rev. 22:14: "Blessed are they that do His commandments, that they may have right to the tree of life, and may enter in through the gates into the city." "Blessed are the undefiled in the way, who walk in the law of the Lord." Ps. 119:1.

So, then, they that are of faith are keepers of the law; for they that are of faith are blessed, and those who do the commandments are blessed. By faith they do the commandments. The Gospel is contrary to human nature, and so it is that we become doers of the law, not by doing, but by believing. If we worked for righteousness, we should be exercising only our own sinful human nature, and so would get no nearer to righteousness, but farther from it; but by believing the "exceeding great and precious promises," we become partakers of the Divine nature (2 Pet. 1:4), and then all our works are wrought in God. "The Gentiles, which followed not after righteousness, have attained to righteousness, even the righteousness which is of faith. But Israel, which followed after the law of righteousness, hath not attained to the law of righteousness. Wherefore?—Because they sought it not by faith, but as it were by the works of the law. For they stumbled at that {109} stumbling-stone;–stone; as it is written, Behold, I lay in Sion a Stumbling-stone and Rock of offense; and whosoever believeth on Him shall not be ashamed." Rom. 9:30–33.

What the Curse Is

No one can read Gal. 3:10 carefully and thoughtfully without seeing that the curse is transgression of the law. Disobedience to God's law is itself the curse; for "by one man sin entered into the world, and death by sin." Rom. 5:12. Sin has death wrapped up in it. Without sin death would be impossible, for "the sting of death is sin." 1 Cor. 15:56. "As many as are of the works of the law are under the curse." Why? Is it because the law is a curse?—Not by any means. "The law is holy, and the commandment holy, and just, and good." Rom. 7:12. Why, then, are as many as are of the works of the law under the curse?—Because it is written, "Cursed is every one that continueth not in all things which are written in the book of the law to do them." Mark it well: They are not cursed because they do the law, but because they do not do it. So, then, we see that being of the works of the law does not mean that one is doing the law. No; "the carnal mind is enmity against God; for it is not subject to the law of God, neither indeed can be." Rom. 8:7. All are under the curse, and he who thinks to get out by his own works, remains there. The curse consists in not continuing in all things that are written in the law; therefore, the blessing means perfect conformity to the law. This is as plain as language can make it. {110}

Blessing and Cursing

"Behold, I set before you this day a blessing and a curse; a blessing, if ye obey the commandments of the Lord your God, which I command you this day; and a curse, if ye will not obey the commandments of the Lord your God." Deut. 11:26–28. This is the living word of God, addressed to each one of us personally. "The law worketh wrath" (Rom. 4:15), but the wrath of God comes only on the children of disobedience (Eph. 5:6). If we truly believe, we are not condemned, but only because faith brings us into harmony with the law—the life of God. "Whoso looketh into the perfect law of liberty, and continueth therein, he being not a forgetful hearer, but a doer of the work, this man shall be blessed in his deed." Jam. 1:25.

Good Works

The Bible does not disparage good works. On the contrary, it exalts them. "This is a faithful saying, and these things I will that thou affirm constantly, that they which have believed in God might be careful to maintain good works. These things are good and profitable." Titus 3:8. The charge against the unbelieving is that they are "unto every good work reprobate." Titus 1:16. Timothy was exhorted to "charge them that are rich in this world," "that they do good, that they be rich in good works." 1 Tim. 6:17,18. And the apostle Paul prayed for us all, that we might "walk worthy of the Lord unto all pleasing, being fruitful in every good work." Col. 1:10. Still further, we are assured that

God has {111} created us in Christ Jesus "unto good works," "that we should walk in them." Eph. 2:10.

He has Himself prepared these works for us, wrought them out, and laid them up for all who trust in Him. Ps. 31:19. "This is the work of God, that ye believe on Him whom He hath sent." n 6:29. Good works are commended, but we can not do them. They can be performed only by the One who is good, and that is God. If there be ever any good in us, it is God who worketh in us. There is no disparagement of anything that He does. "Now the God of peace, that brought again from the dead our Lord Jesus, that great Shepherd of the sheep, through the blood of the everlasting covenant, make you perfect in every good work to do His will, working in you that which is well pleasing in His sight, through Jesus Christ; to whom be glory forever and ever. Amen." Heb. 13:20,21.

Who Are the Just?

When we read the frequent statement, "The just shall live by faith," it is necessary to have a clear idea of what the word "just" means. If we read the same text in the Revised Version, we shall learn. It has it, "The righteous shall live by faith." To be justified by faith is to be made righteous by faith. "All unrighteousness is sin" (1 n. 5:17), and "sin is the transgression of the law" (1 n. 3:4). Therefore, all unrighteousness is transgression of the law, and of course all righteousness is obedience to the law. So we see that the just, or righteous, man is the man who obeys the law, and to be justified is to be made a keeper of the law. {112}

How to Become Just

Righteousness is the end to be obtained, and the law of God is the standard. "The law worketh wrath," because "all have sinned," and "the wrath of God cometh on the children of disobedience." How shall we become doers of the law, and thus escape wrath, or the curse? The answer is, "The righteous shall live by faith." By faith, not by works, we become doers of the law. "With the heart man believeth unto righteousness." Rom. 10:10. That no man is justified by the law in the sight of God, it is evident. From what does it appear?—From this,—that "the just shall live by faith." If righteousness came by works, then it would not be by faith; "if by grace, then is it no more of works; otherwise grace is no more grace." Rom. 11:6. "To him that worketh is the reward not reckoned of grace, but of debt. But to him that worketh not, but believeth on Him that justifieth the ungodly, his faith is counted for righteousness." Rom. 4:4,5. There is no exception, no half-way working. It is not said that some of the just shall live by faith, or that they shall live by faith and works, but, simply, "the just shall live by faith," and that proves that it is not by their own works. All of the just are made and kept just by faith alone. This is because the law is so holy. It is greater than can be done by man; only Divine power can accomplish it; so by faith we receive the Lord Jesus, and He lives the perfect law in us.

The Law Not of Faith

"The law is not of faith." Of course it is the written law, no matter whether in a book or on tables of stone, that is here referred to. That law simply {113} says, "Do this," or, "Do not do that." "The man that doeth them shall live in them." That is the sole condition on which the written law offers life. Works, and works only, commend themselves to it. How those works are obtained is of no consequence to it, provided they are present. But none have done the requirements of the law, and so there can be no doers of the law, that is, none who in their own lives can present a record of perfect obedience.

Life Is Action

"The man that doeth them shall live in them." But one must be alive in order to do. A dead man can do nothing, and he who is "dead in trespasses and sins" can do no righteousness. Christ is the only one in whom there is life, for He is the life, and He alone has done and can do the righteousness of the law. When, instead of being denied and repressed, He is acknowledged and received, He lives in us all the fullness of His life, so that it is no more we but Christ living in us, and then His obedience in us makes us righteous. Our faith is counted for righteousness, simply because our faith appropriates the living Christ. In trust we yield our bodies as temples of God; Christ, the Living Stone, is enshrined in the heart, which becomes God's throne, and so the living law is our life; for out of the heart are the issues of life.

The Real Question at Issue

Let the reader pay particular attention to the fact that there is in this epistle no controversy over the law, as to whether or not it should be obeyed. No one had claimed that the law was {114} abolished, or changed, or had lost its force. The epistle contains no hint of any such thing. The question was not if the law should be kept, but how it was to be kept. Justification—being made righteous—was admitted to be a necessity; the question was, Is it by faith, or by works? The false brethren were persuading the Galatians that they must be made righteous by their own efforts; Paul was by the Spirit showing that all such attempts were useless, and could result only in fastening more firmly the curse upon the sinner. Righteousness through faith in Jesus Christ is set forth to all men in all time as the only real righteousness. The false teachers made their boast in the law, but through breaking it caused the name of God to be blasphemed. Paul made his boast in Christ, and by the righteousness of the law, to which he thus submitted, caused the name of God to be glorified in him.

The Sting of Sin

That death is the curse is evident from the last part of verse 13, "Cursed is every one that hangeth on a tree." Christ was made a curse for us, in that He hung on a tree, that is, was crucified. But sin is the cause of death. "By one man sin entered into the world, and death by sin; and so death passed upon all men, for that all have sinned." Rom. 5:12. "The sting of death is sin." 1 Cor. 15:56. So we have the substance of verse 10 thus, that those who do not continue in the things written in the law are dead. That is, disobedience is death. And this is what the Scripture says: "When lust hath conceived, it bringeth {115} forth sin; and sin, when it is finished, bringeth forth death." Sin contains death, and men out of Christ are "dead in trespasses and sins." It matters not that they walk about seemingly full of life, the words of Christ are, "Except ye eat the flesh of the Son of man, and drink His blood, ye have no life in you." n 6:53. "She that liveth in pleasure is dead while she liveth." 1 Tim. 5:6. It is a living death—a body of death—that is endured. Rom. 7:24. Sin is the transgression of the law; the wages of sin is death. The curse, therefore, is the death that is carried about concealed even in the most attractive sin. "Cursed is every one that continueth not in all things which are written in the book of the law to do them."

Redemption from the Curse

"Christ hath redeemed us from the curse of the law." Let us stop right here and contemplate this fact, leaving the way of redemption for later consideration. We need to consider the statement very carefully, for some who read it straightway rush off frantically exclaiming, "We don't need to keep the law, because Christ has redeemed us from the curse of it," as though the text said that Christ redeemed us from the curse of obedience. Such read the Scriptures to no profit. The curse, as we have seen it, is disobedience. "Cursed is every one that continueth not in all things which are written in the book of the law to do them." Therefore, Christ has redeemed us from disobedience to the law. God sent forth His Son in the likeness of sinful flesh, and {116} for sin, "that the righteousness of the law might be fulfilled in us." Rom. 8:4.

Some one may lightly say, "Then we are all right; whatever we do is right so far as the law is concerned, since we are redeemed." It is true that all are redeemed, but not all have accepted redemption. Many say of Christ, "We will not have this

Man to reign over us," and thrust the blessing of God from them. But redemption is for all; all have been purchased with the precious blood—the life—of Christ, and all may be, if they will, free from sin and death. By that blood we are redeemed from our "vain manner of life." 1 Pet. 1:18, R.V.

Stop and think what this means; let the full force of the announcement impress itself upon your consciousness. "Christ hath redeemed us from the curse of the law,"—from not continuing in all its righteous requirements. We need not sin any more. He has snapped asunder the cords of sin that bound us, so that we have but to accept His salvation in order to be free from every besetting sin. It is not necessary for us any longer to spend our lives in earnest longings for a better life, and in vain regrets for desires unrealized. Christ raises no false hopes, but He comes to the captives of sin, and cries to them, "Liberty! Your prison doors are open. Go forth." What more can be said? Christ has gained the complete victory over "this present evil world," over "the lust of the flesh, and the lust of the eyes, and the pride of life," and our faith in Him makes His victory ours. We have but to accept it. {117}

Christ Made a Curse for Us

That "Christ died for the ungodly" is evident to all who read the Bible. He "was delivered for our offenses." Rom. 4:25. The Innocent suffered for the guilty; the Just for the unjust. "He was wounded for our transgressions, He was bruised for our iniquities; the chastisement of our peace was upon Him; and with His stripes we are healed. All we like sheep have gone astray; we have turned every one to his own way; and the Lord hath laid on Him the iniquity of us all." Is. 53:5,6. But death came by sin. Death is the curse that has passed upon all men, simply because "all have sinned." So, as Christ was "made a curse for us," it follows that Christ was "made to be sin on our behalf." 2 Cor. 5:21, R.V. He bore "our sins in His own body" up to the tree. 1 Pet. 2:24, margin. Note that our sins were "in His body." It was no superficial work that He undertook. The sins were not merely figuratively laid on Him, but they were actually in Him. He was made a curse for us, made to be sin for us, and consequently suffered death for us.

To some this truth seems repugnant; to the Greeks it is foolishness, and to the Jews a stumbling-block, but "to us who are saved, it is the power of God." For bear in mind that it was our sins that He bore in His own body—not His own sins. The same scripture that tells us that He was made to be sin for us, assures us that He "knew no sin." The same text that tells us that He carried our sins "in His own body," is careful to let us know that He {118} "did no sin." The fact that He could carry our sin about with Him, and in Him, being actually made to be sin for us, and yet not do any sin, is to His everlasting glory and our eternal salvation from sin. All the sins of all men were on Him, yet no person ever discovered the trace of sin upon Him. No sin was ever manifested in His life, although He took all sin upon Himself. He received it and swallowed it up by the power of the endless life in which He swallows up death. He can bear sin, and yet be untainted by it. It is by this marvelous life that He redeems us. He gives us His life, so that we may be freed from every taint of the sin that is in our flesh.

Christ, "in the days of His flesh, when He had offered up prayers and supplications with strong crying and tears unto Him that was able to save Him from death," "was heard in that He feared." Heb. 5:7. But He died! Yes; but no one took His life from Him; He laid it down, that He might take it again. n 10:17,18. The pangs of death were loosed, "because it was not possible that He should be holden of it." Acts 2:24. Why was it not possible for death to hold Him, even though He voluntarily put Himself in its power?—Because He "knew no sin;" He took sin upon Himself, but was saved from its power. He was "in all things" "made like unto His brethren," "in all points tempted like as we are" (Heb. 2:17; 4:15), and since He could of Himself do nothing (n 5:30), He prayed to the Father to keep Him from being overcome and thereby falling under the power of death. And He was heard. In His case these words were fulfilled: "The Lord God will help {119} Mc; therefore shall I not be confounded; therefore have I set My face like a flint, and I know that I shall not be ashamed. He is near that justifieth Me; who will contend with Me?" Is. 50:7,8.

Whose sin was it that thus oppressed Him, and from which He was delivered?—Not His own, for He had none. It was your sin and mine. Our sins have already been overcome—vanquished. We have to fight only with an already defeated foe. When you come to God "in the name of Jesus," having surrendered yourself to His death and life, so that you do not bear His name in vain, because Christ liveth in you, you have only to remember that every sin was on Him, and is still on Him, and that He is the conqueror, and straightway you will say, "Thanks be to God, which giveth us the victory through our Lord Jesus Christ." "Now thanks be unto God, which always causeth us to triumph in Christ, and maketh manifest the savor of His knowledge by us in every place." 2 Cor. 2:14.

The Revelation of the Cross

In Gal. 3:13 we are brought back to the subject presented in Gal. 2:20 and 3:1,—the ever-present cross. The subject is inexhaustible, but the following few facts may serve to open it up to our minds:—

1. The redemption from sin and death is accomplished through the cross. Gal. 3:13.

2. The Gospel is all contained in the cross; for the Gospel is "the power of God unto salvation to every one that believeth" (Rom. 1:16), and "unto us which {120} are saved" the cross of Christ "is the power of God" (1 Cor. 1:18).

3. Christ is revealed to fallen men only as the Crucified and risen One. There is none other name under heaven given among men, whereby salvation may be obtained (Acts 4:12), and, therefore, it is all that God sets forth before men, since He does not wish to confuse them. "Christ and Him crucified," is all that Paul wished to know; it is all that any man needs to know. Thus the one thing that men need is salvation; if they get that, they get all things; but salvation is found only in the cross of Christ; therefore, God puts before the eyes of men nothing else: He gives them just what they need. Jesus Christ is by God set forth openly crucified before the eyes of every man, so that there is no excuse for any to be lost, or to continue in sin.

4. Christ is set forth before men only as the crucified Redeemer; and since that from which men need to be saved is the curse, He is set forth as bearing the curse. Wherever there is any curse, there is Christ bearing it. We have already seen that Christ bore, and still bears, our curse, in that He bears our sin. He also bears the curse of the earth itself, for He bore the crown of thorns, and the curse pronounced on the earth was, "Thorns also and thistles shall it bring forth." Gen. 3:18. So the whole creation, which now groans under the curse, has been redeemed through the cross of Christ. Rom. 8:19–23.

5. It is only on the cross that Christ bears the curse, for His being made a curse for us was indicated by {121} His hanging on the cross. The cross is the symbol of the curse, but also of deliverance from the curse, since it is the cross of Christ, the Conqueror and Deliverer. The very curse itself, therefore, presents the cross, and proclaims our deliverance.

6. Where is the curse? Ah, where is it not? The blindest can see it, if he will but acknowledge the evidence of his own senses. Imperfection is a curse, yea, that is the curse; and imperfection is on everything connected with this earth. Man is imperfect, and even the finest plant that grows from the earth is not as perfect as it might be. There is nothing that meets the eye that does not show the possibility of improvement, even if our untrained eyes can not see the absolute necessity of it. When God made the earth, everything was "very good," or, as the Hebrew idiom has it, "good exceedingly." God Himself could see no chance, no possibility, for improvement. But now it is

different. The gardener spends his thought and labor trying to improve the fruits and flowers under his care. And since the best that the earth produces reveals the curse, what need be said of the gnarled, stunted growths, the withered and blasted buds and leaves and fruits, and the noxious, poisonous weeds? Everywhere "hath the curse devoured the earth." Is. 24:6.

7. What, then, is the conclusion of the whole matter? Is it discouragement? Nay; "for God hath not appointed us to wrath, but to obtain salvation by our Lord Jesus Christ." 1Thess. 5:9.

Although the curse is visible everywhere,—

"Change and decay in all around I see,"—

{122} yet things live, and men live. But the curse is death, and no man and no thing in creation can bear death and still live. Death kills. But Christ is He that liveth, and was dead, and is alive forevermore. Rev. 1:18. He alone can bear the curse—death—and still live. Therefore, the fact that there is life on the earth and in man, in spite of the curse, is proof that the cross of Christ is everywhere. Every blade of grass, every leaf of the forest, every shrub and tree, every flower and fruit, even the bread that we eat, is stamped with the cross of Christ. In our own bodies is Christ crucified. Everywhere is that cross; and as the preaching of the cross is the power of God, which is the Gospel, so it is that the everlasting power of God is revealed in all things that He has made. That is "the power that worketh in us." Eph. 3:20. Rom. 1:16–20, compared with 1 Cor. 1:17,18, amounts to a plain declaration that the cross of Christ is seen in all the things that God has made—even in our own bodies.

Courage from Despair

"Innumerable evils have compassed me about; mine iniquities have taken hold upon me, so that I am not able to look up; they are more than the hairs of mine head; therefore my heart faileth me." Ps. 40:12. But not only may we with confidence cry unto God out of the depths, but God in His infinite mercy has so ordered it that the very depths themselves are a source of confidence. The fact that we are in the depths of sin, and yet live, is proof that God Himself, in the person of Christ on the cross, is present with us to deliver us. So everything, {123} even the curse, for everything is under the curse, preaches the Gospel. Our own weakness and sinfulness, instead of being a cause of discouragement, are, if we believe the Lord, a pledge of redemption. Out of weakness we are made strong. "In all these things we are more than conquerors through Him that loved us." Rom. 8:37. Truly, God has not left Himself without witness among men. "He that believeth on the Son of God hath the witness in himself." 1 . 5:10.

The Blessing from the Curse

Christ bore the curse, in order that the blessing might come
to us. He bears the curse now, being crucified before us, and in
us, and we with Him, that we may continually experience the
blessing. Death to Him is life to us. If we willingly bear about
in our bodies the dying of the Lord Jesus, the life also of Jesus
will be manifested in our mortal flesh. 2 Cor. 4:10,11. He {199}
was made to be sin for us, that we might be made the righteousness of God in Him. 2 Cor. 5:21. What is the blessing that we
receive through the curse that He bears? It is the blessing of
salvation from sin; for as the curse is the transgression of the
law (Gal. 3:10), the blessing consists in turning away every one
of us from our iniquities (Acts 3:26). Christ suffered the curse,
even sin and death, "that the blessing of Abraham might come
on the Gentiles through Jesus Christ." And what is the blessing
of Abraham? The writer of this Epistle, having stated that
Abraham was made righteous by faith, adds: "Even as David
also describeth the blessedness of the man, {124} unto whom
God imputeth righteousness without works, saying, Blessed are
they whose iniquities are forgiven, and whose sins are covered.
Blessed is the man to whom the Lord will not impute sin." Rom.
4:6–8. And then he shows that this blessing comes on the
Gentiles as well as on the Jews who believe, because Abraham
received it when he was uncircumcised, "that he might be the
father of all them that believe." The blessing is freedom from
sin, even as the curse is the doing of sin; and as the curse reveals
the cross, so we find that the very curse is by the Lord made to
proclaim the blessing. The fact that we live, although we are
sinners, is the assurance that deliverance from the sin is ours.
"While there's life there's hope," says the adage. Yes, because
the Life is our hope. Thank God for the blessed hope! The
blessing has come upon all men; for "as by the offense of one
judgment came upon all men to condemnation; even so by the
righteousness of One the free gift came upon all men unto
justification of life." Rom. 5:18. God, who is "no respecter of
persons," "hath blessed us with all spiritual blessings in heavenly places in Christ." Eph. 1:3. It is ours to keep. If any one has
not this blessing, it is because he has not recognized the gift, or
has deliberately thrown it away.

A Finished Work

"Christ hath redeemed us from the curse of the law,"—from
sin and death. This He has done by "being made a curse for us,"
and so we are freed from all necessity of sinning. Sin can have
no dominion {125} over us if we accept Christ in truth, and
without reserve. This was just as much a present truth in the
days of Abraham, Moses, David, and Isaiah, as it is to-day. More

than seven hundred years before the cross was raised on Calvary, Isaiah, who testified of the things which he understood, because his own sin had been purged by a live coal from God's altar, said: "Surely He hath borne our griefs, and carried our sorrows;...He wasHe was wounded for our transgressions, He was bruised for our iniquities; the chastisement of our peace was upon Him; and with His stripes we are healed.... The Lord hath laid on Him the iniquity of us all." Is. 53:4–6. "I have blotted out, as a thick cloud, thy transgressions, and, as a cloud, thy sins; return unto Me; for I have redeemed thee." Is. 44:22. Long before Isaiah's time, David wrote: "He hath not dealt with us after our sins; nor rewarded us according to our iniquities." "As far as the east is from the west, so far hath He removed our transgressions from us." Ps. 103:10,12.

"We which have believed do enter into rest," because "the works were finished from the foundation of the world." Heb. 4:3. The blessing that we received is "the blessing of Abraham." We have no other foundation than that of the apostles and prophets. Eph. 2:20. It is a full and complete salvation that God has provided; it awaits us as we come into the world; and we do not relieve God of any burden by rejecting it, nor do we add to His labor by accepting it. {126}

"The Promise of the Spirit"

Christ hath redeemed us, "that we might receive the promise of the Spirit through faith." Do not make the mistake of reading this as though it were "that we might receive the promise of the gift of the Spirit." It does not say that, and it does not mean that, as a little thought will show. Christ has redeemed us, and that fact proves the gift of the Spirit, for it was only "through the eternal Spirit" that He offered Himself without spot to God. Heb. 9:14. But for the Spirit, we should not know that we were sinners; much less should we know redemption. The Spirit convinces of sin and of righteousness. n 16:8. "It is the Spirit that beareth witness, because the Spirit is truth." 1 . 5:6. "He that believeth hath the witness in himself." Christ is crucified in every man; that, as we have already seen, is shown in the fact that we are all under the curse, and Christ alone, on the cross, bears the curse. But it is through the Spirit that Christ dwells on earth among men. Faith enables us to receive the testimony of this witness, and rejoice in that which the possession of the Spirit assures.

Note further: The blessing of Abraham comes on us, in order that we may receive the promise of the Spirit. But it is only through the Spirit that the blessing comes; therefore, the blessing can not bring to us the promise that we shall receive the Spirit. We already have the Spirit with the blessing. But, having the blessing of the Spirit, namely, righteousness, we are sure of receiving that which the Spirit promises to the righteous, namely, an everlasting {127} inheritance. In blessing Abraham God promised him an inheritance. The expression, "the promise of the Spirit," is used, as is plainly to be seen, in the same sense as "the promise of God," "the gift of God;" that is, the promise or the gift which God bestows. The Spirit is the pledge of all good.

The Spirit the Pledge of Inheritance

All God's gifts are in themselves promises of more. There is always much more to follow. God's purpose in the Gospel is to gather together in one all things in Jesus Christ, "in whom also we have obtained an inheritance, being predestinated according to the purpose of Him who worketh all things after the counsel of His own will; that we should be to the praise of His glory, who first trusted in Christ. In whom ye also trusted, after that ye heard the Word of truth, the Gospel of your salvation; in whom also after that [or when] ye believed, ye were sealed with that Holy Spirit of promise, which is the earnest of our inheritance until the redemption of the purchased possession, unto the praise of His glory." Eph. 1:10–14.

Of this inheritance we must speak further later on. Suffice it now to say that it is the inheritance promised to Abraham, whose children we become by faith. The inheritance belongs to all who are children of God through faith in Christ Jesus; and the Spirit that marks our sonship is the promise, the pledge, the first-fruits of that inheritance. Those who accept Christ's glorious deliverance from the curse of the law,—redemption not from obedience to the law, for obedience is not a curse, but from disobedience to the {128} law,—have in the Spirit a taste of the power and the blessing of the world to come.

The Promise Was Made to Abraham

It will be seen that Abraham is the one about whom this chapter centers. He is the one to whom the Gospel of world-wide salvation was preached. He believed, and received the blessing, even the blessing of righteousness. All who believe are blessed with believing Abraham. They who are of faith, the same are the children of Abraham. Christ hath redeemed us from the curse, in order that the blessing of Abraham might come on us. "To Abraham and his seed were the promises made." "If the inheritance be of the law, it is no more of promise; but God gave it to Abraham by promise." Thus it is clear that the promise to us is the promise that was made to Abraham,—the promise of an inheritance,—and in which we share as his children. Christ hath redeemed us from the curse, that we might receive the inheritance of righteousness. Christ through the eternal Spirit offered Himself without spot to God, to purge our consciences from dead works to serve the living God; because "He is the Mediator of the new covenant, that by means of death...they which are called might receive the promise of eternal inheritance." Heb. 9:14,15.

"And His Seed"

"Now to Abraham and his seed were the promises made. He saith not, And to seeds, as of many; but as of one; and to thy Seed, which is Christ." There is{129} here no play upon words; the issue is a vital one. The controversy is over the way of salvation, whether it is by Christ alone, or by something else, or by Christ and something or somebody else. Many people imagine that it is by them,—that they must save themselves by making themselves good. Many others think that Christ is a valuable adjunct, a good assistant to their efforts; while others still are willing to give Him the first place, but not the only place. They regard themselves as good seconds. It is the Lord and they who do the work. But our text shuts off all this assumption and self-assertion. Not seeds, but the seed. Not many, but one. "And to thy Seed, which is Christ." Christ is the One.

Not Two Lines

We hear much about the "spiritual seed" and the "literal seed" of Abraham. If that contrast meant anything at all, it would mean a fanciful seed as opposed to a real seed. The opposite of spiritual is fleshly, and the fleshly seed, as we shall see later on, is not the real seed, but only a bond-servant, to be cast out, having no share whatever in the inheritance. So there is no fleshly seed of Abraham. The spiritual seed, however, is a literal, or real, seed, even as Christ is "a quickening Spirit," and yet most real. It is possible for men walking about in the body, in this world, to be wholly spiritual, and such they must be, or else they are not children of Abraham. "They that are in the flesh can not please God." "Flesh and blood doth not inherit the kingdom of God." There is only one line of descendants from Abraham, only one set of real children, and they are those who are {130} of faith,—those who, by receiving Christ by faith, receive power to become sons of God.

Many Promises in One

But while the Seed is singular, the promises are plural. It is not merely one specific promise that was made to Abraham and his Seed, but promises. God has nothing for any man that was not promised to Abraham; and all the promises of God are conveyed in Christ, in whom Abraham believed. "For how many soever be the promises of God, in Him is the yea; wherefore also through Him is the Amen, unto the glory of God through us." 2 Cor. 1:20.

The Promised Inheritance

That the thing promised, and the sum of all the promises, is an inheritance, is clearly seen from Gal. 3:15–18. The sixteenth verse has just been noted, and the seventeenth verse tells us that the law, coming in four hundred and thirty years after the promise was made and confirmed, can not make it of none effect; "for if the inheritance be of the law, it is no more of promise; but God gave it to Abraham by promise." Verse 18. What this promised inheritance is may be seen by comparing the verse just quoted with Rom. 4:13: "For the promise, that he should be the heir of the world, was not to Abraham, or to his seed, through the law, but through the righteousness of faith." And so, although the heavens and the earth which are now are "reserved unto fire against the day of judgment and perdition of ungodly men," when "the heavens being on fire shall be dissolved, and the elements shall melt with fervent {131} heat," we, "according to His promise, look for new heavens and a new earth, wherein dwelleth righteousness." 2 Pet. 3:7,12,13. This is the heavenly country for which Abraham, Isaac, and Jacob looked.

An Inheritance without Curse

"Christ hath redeemed us from the curse;...that we might receive the promise of the Spirit through faith." This "promise of the Spirit" we have seen to be the possession of the whole earth made new—redeemed from the curse; for "the creation itself also shall be delivered from the bondage of corruption into the liberty of the glory of the children of God." The earth, fresh and new from the hand of God, perfect in every respect, was given to man for a possession. Gen. 1:27,28,31. Man sinned, and brought the curse upon himself. Christ has taken the whole curse, both of man and of all creation, upon Himself. He redeems the earth from the curse, that it may be the everlasting possession that God originally designed it to be, and He also redeems man from the curse, that he may be fitted for the possession of such an inheritance. This is the sum of the Gospel. "The gift of God is eternal life through Jesus Christ our Lord." Rom. 6:23. This gift of eternal life is included in the promise of the inheritance, for God promised the land to Abraham and to his seed for "an everlasting possession." Gen. 17:7,8. It is an inheritance of righteousness, because the promise that Abraham should be heir of the world was through the righteousness of faith. Righteousness, eternal life, and a place in which to live eternally,—these are all in the promise, and they {132} are all that could possibly be desired or given. To redeem man, but to give him no place in which to live, would be an incomplete work; the two things are parts of one whole, for the power by which we are redeemed is the power of creation,—the power by which the heavens and the earth are made new. When all is accomplished, "there shall be no more curse." Rev. 22:3.

The Covenants of Promise

That the covenant and promise of God are one and the same thing, is clearly seen from Gal. 3:17, where it appears that to disannul the covenant would be to make void the promise. In Genesis 17 we read that God made a covenant with Abraham to give him the land of Canaan—and with it the whole world—for an everlasting possession; but Gal. 3:18 says that God gave it to him by promise. God's covenants with men can be nothing else than promises to them: "Who hath first given to Him, and it shall be recompensed unto him again? For of Him, and through Him, and to Him, are all things." Rom. 11:35,36. It is so rare for men to do anything without expecting an equivalent, that theologians have taken it for granted that it is the same with God. So they begin their dissertations on God's covenant with the statement that a covenant is "a mutual agreement between two or more persons, to do or refrain from doing certain things." But God does not make bargains with men, because He knows that they could not fulfill their part. After the flood God made a covenant with every beast of {133} the earth, and with every fowl; but the beasts and the birds did not promise anything in return. Gen. 9:9–16. They simply received the favor at the hand of God. That is all we can do. God promises us everything that we need, and more than we can ask or think, as a gift. We give Him ourselves, that is, nothing, and He gives us Himself, that is, everything. That which makes all the trouble is that even when men are willing to recognize the Lord at all, they want to make bargains with Him. They want it to be a "mutual" affair—a transaction in which they will be considered as on a par with God. But whoever deals with God must deal with Him on His own terms, that is, on a basis of fact—that we have nothing and are nothing, and He has everything and is everything, and gives everything.

The Covenant Confirmed

The covenant, that is, the promise of God to give men the whole earth made new, after having made them free from the curse, was "confirmed before of God in Christ." He is the Surety of the new covenant, even the everlasting covenant. "For how many soever be the promises of God, in Him is the yea; wherefore also through Him is the Amen, unto the glory of God through us." 2 Cor. 1:20, R.V. In Him we have obtained the inheritance (Eph. 1:11), for the Holy Spirit is the first-fruits of the inheritance, and the possession of the Holy Spirit is Christ Himself dwelling in the heart by faith. God blessed Abraham, saying, "In thy Seed shall all the kindreds of the earth be blessed," and this is fulfilled in Christ, {134} whom God has sent to bless us in turning us away from our iniquities. Acts 3:25,26.

Confirmed by an Oath of God

"When God made promise to Abraham, because He could swear by no greater, He sware by Himself;...for men verily swear by the greater; and an oath for confirmation is to them an end of all strife. Wherein God, willing more abundantly to show unto the heirs of promise the immutability of His counsel, confirmed it by an oath; that by two immutable things, in which it was impossible for God to lie, we might have a strong consolation, who have fled for refuge to lay hold upon the hope set before us; which hope we have as an anchor of the soul, both sure and steadfast, and which entereth into that within the veil; whither the forerunner is for us entered, even Jesus, made an high priest forever after the order of Melchizedek." Heb. 6:13–20. Compare Gen. 22:15–18.

It was the oath of God, therefore, that confirmed the covenant made to Abraham; that promise and oath to Abraham are our ground of hope, our strong consolation; they are "sure and steadfast," because the oath sets forth Christ as the pledge, the surety, and "He ever liveth." He upholds all things by the word of His power. Heb. 1:3. "In Him all things consist." Col. 1:17, R.V. Therefore, when God "interposed Himself by an oath," which is our consolation and hope in fleeing for refuge from sin, He pledged His own existence, and with it the entire universe, for our salvation. Surely a firm foundation for our hope is laid in His excellent Word. {135}

The Law Can Not Make the Covenant Void

Do not forget as we proceed that the covenant and the promise are the same thing, and that it conveys land, even the whole earth made new, to Abraham and his seed; and remember also that, since only righteousness is to dwell in the new heavens and the new earth promised to Abraham and his seed, the promise includes the making righteous of all who believe. This is done in Christ, in whom the promise is confirmed. Now, "though it be but a man's covenant, yet if it be confirmed, no man disannulleth, or addeth thereto." Gal. 3:15. How much more must this be the case with God's covenant! Therefore, since perfect and everlasting righteousness was assured by the covenant made with Abraham, which was also confirmed in Christ, by the oath of God, it is impossible that the law, which was spoken four hundred and thirty years later, could introduce any new feature. The inheritance was given to Abraham by promise, but if after four hundred and thirty years it should transpire that now the inheritance must be gained in some other way, then the promise would be of no effect, and the covenant would be made void. But that would involve the overthrow of God's government, and the ending of His existence; for He pledged His own existence to give Abraham and his seed the inheritance and the righteousness necessary for it. "For the promise, that he should be the heir of the world, was not to Abraham, or to his seed, through the law, but through the righteousness of faith." Rom. 4:13. The Gospel was as full {136} and complete in the days of Abraham as it has ever been or ever will be. No addition to it, or change in its provisions or conditions, could possibly be made after God's oath to Abraham. Nothing can be taken away from it as it thus existed, and not one thing can ever be required from any man more than what was required of Abraham.

What Is the Use of the Law?

This is the question that the apostle Paul asks in verse 19, both for the purpose of anticipating the objections of the Antinomians, and also that he may the more emphatically show the place of the law in the Gospel. The question is a very natural one. Since the inheritance is wholly by promise, and a covenant confirmed can not be changed,—nothing can be taken from it, and nothing added to it,—why did the law come in four hundred and thirty years afterward? "Wherefore then serveth the law?" More literally, Why then the law? What business has it here? What part does it act? Of what use is it?

The Question Answered

"It was added because of transgressions." Let it be understood that "the entering of the law" at Sinai was not the beginning of its existence. The law of God existed in the days of Abraham, and was kept by him. Gen. 26:5. God proved the children of Israel, as to whether they would keep His law or not, more than a month before the law was spoken upon Sinai. Ex. 16:1–4,27,28. {137}

"It Was Added"

The word here rendered "added" is the same as that rendered "spoken" in Heb. 12:19: "They that heard entreated that the word should not be spoken to them any more." It is the same word that occurs in the Septuagint rendering of Deut. 5:22, where we read that God spoke the ten commandments with a great voice; "and He added no more." So we may read the answer to the question, "Wherefore then the law?" thus: "It was spoken because of transgressions." It is the reprover of sin.

Because of Transgressions

"Moreover the law entered, that the offense might abound."
Rom. 5:20. In other words, "that sin by the commandment
might become exceeding sinful." Rom. 7:13. It was given under
circumstances of the most awful majesty, as a warning to the
children of Israel that by their unbelief they were in danger of
losing the promised inheritance. They did not, like Abraham,
believe the Lord; and "whatsoever is not of faith is sin." But the
inheritance was promised "through the righteousness of faith,"
and, therefore, the unbelieving Jews could not receive it. So the
law was spoken to them, to convince them that they had not the
righteousness that was necessary for the possession of the
inheritance; for, although righteousness does not come by the
law, it must be witnessed by the law. Rom. 3:21. In short, the
law was given to show them that they had not faith, and so were
not true children of Abraham, and were therefore in a fair way
to lose {138} the inheritance. God would have put His law into
their hearts, even as He put it into Abraham's heart, if they had
believed; but when they disbelieved, yet still professed to be
heirs of the promise, it was necessary to show them in the most
marked manner that their unbelief was sin. The law was spoken
because of transgression, or, what is the same thing, because of
the unbelief of the people.

Self-Confidence Is Sin

"Behold, his soul which is lifted up is not upright in him; but
the just shall live by his faith." Hab. 2:4. The people of Israel
were full of self-confidence and of unbelief in God, as is shown
by their murmuring against God's leading, and by their assumption of ability to do anything that God required, or to fulfill His
promises. They had the same spirit as their descendants, who
asked, "What shall we do, that we might work the works of
God?" n 6:28. They were so ignorant of God's righteousness that
they thought that they could establish their own righteousness
as an equivalent. Rom. 10:3. Unless they saw their sin, they
could not avail themselves of the promise. Hence, the necessity
of the speaking of the law.

The Ministration of Angels

"Are they not all ministering spirits, sent forth to do service
for the sake of them that shall inherit salvation?" Heb. 1:14, R.V.
Just what office the "thousands of angels" who were at Sinai
had to perform, we can not know; but we do know {139} that
they have a close and deep interest in everything that concerns
man, although the preaching of the Gospel is necessarily not
committed to them. When the foundations of the earth were
laid, "all the sons of God shouted for joy;" and a multitude of

the heavenly host sang praises when the birth of the Saviour of mankind was announced. They are attendants upon the King of kings, waiting to "do His pleasure, harkening unto the voice of His word." It would not be otherwise than that they should attend as a royal body-guard when the law was proclaimed, and, of course, they were not there merely for pomp and parade. Stephen said to the murderous Sanhedrim: "Ye stiff-necked and uncircumcised in heart and ears, ye do always resist the Holy Ghost; as your fathers did, so do ye. Which of the prophets have not your fathers persecuted? and they have slain them which showed before of the coming of the Just One; of whom ye have been now the betrayers and murderers; who have received the law by the disposition of angels, and have not kept it." Acts 7:51–53. Of him who is now the adversary, the devil, it was said, "Thou sealest up the sum," measure, or pattern. Eze. 28:12. The French of Segond has it, "Thou puttest the seal to perfection," and the Danish, "Thou stampest the seal upon the fit ordinance," indicating that before his fall he was what might be termed the keeper of the seal, and that it was his duty to affix it to every ordinance passed. Angels "excel in strength," and the fact that they were all present at the giving of the law shows that it was an event of the greatest magnitude and importance. {140}

In the Hand of a Mediator

For the present we may pass by the question of time involved in the phrase, "till the Seed should come, to whom the promise was made," since our present study is the relation of the law to the promise. The law was given to the people from Sinai "in the hand of a Mediator." Who was this Mediator?—There can be only one answer: "There is one God, and one Mediator between God and men, the Man Christ Jesus." 1 Tim. 2:5. "Now a mediator is not a mediator of one, but God is one." God is one, the people are the other, and Christ Jesus is the Mediator. Just as surely as God is one party to the transaction, Christ must be the Mediator, for there is no other mediator between God and men. "Neither is there salvation in any other; for there is none other name under heaven given among men, whereby we must be saved." Acts 4:12.

Christ's Work as Mediator

Man has wandered from God, and rebelled against Him. "All we like sheep have gone astray." Our iniquities have separated between us and Him. Is. 59:1,2. "The carnal mind is enmity against God; for it is not subject to the law of God, neither indeed can be." Rom. 8:7. Christ came that He might destroy the enmity, and reconcile us to God; for He is our peace. Eph. 2:14–16. Christ "suffered for sins, the Just for the unjust, that

He might bring us to God." 1 Pet. 3:18. Through Him we have access to God. Rom. 5:1,2; Eph. 2:18. {141}

In Him the carnal mind, the rebellious mind, is taken away, and the mind of the Spirit given in its stead, "that the righteousness of the law might be fulfilled in us, who walk not after the flesh, but after the Spirit." Rom. 8:3,4. Christ's work is to save that which was lost, to restore that which was broken, to reunite that which was separated. His name is "God with us;" and so with Him dwelling in us we are made "partakers of the Divine nature." 2 Pet. 1:4.

It should be understood that Christ's work as Mediator is not limited either as to time or extent. To be Mediator means more than to be intercessor. Christ was Mediator before sin came into the world, and will be Mediator when no sin is in the universe, and no need for expiation. "In Him all things consist." He is the very impress of the Father's being. He is the life. Only in and through Him does the life of God flow to all creation. He is, then, the means, medium, mediator, the way, by which the light of life pervades the universe. He did not first become Mediator at the fall of man, but was such from eternity. No one, not simply no man, but no created being, comes to the Father but by Christ. No angel can stand in the Divine presence except in Christ. No new power was developed, no new machinery, so to speak, was required to be set in motion by the entering of sin into the world. The power that had created all things only continued in God's infinite mercy, to work for the restoration of that which was lost. In Christ were all things created, and, therefore, in Him we {142} have redemption through His blood. Col. 1:14–17. The power that pervades and upholds the universe is the power that saves us. "Now unto Him that is able to do exceeding abundantly above all that we ask or think, according to the power that worketh in us, unto Him be glory in the church by Christ Jesus throughout all ages, world without end. Amen."

The Law Not against the Promise

"Is the law then against the promises of God?"—Not by any means. Far from it. If it were, it would not be in the hands of a Mediator, Christ; for all the promises of God are in Him. 2 Cor. 1:20. So we find the law and the promise combined in Christ. We may know that the law was not and is not against the promises of God, from the fact that God gave both the promise and the law. We know, also, that the giving of the law introduced no new element into the covenant, since, having been confirmed, nothing could be added to or taken from it. But the law is not useless, else God would not have given it. It is not a matter of indifference whether we keep it or not, for God commands it. But, all the same, it is not against the promise, and brings no

new element in. Why?—Simply because the law is in the promise. The promise of the Spirit includes this: "I will put My laws
into their mind, and write them in their hearts." Heb. 8:10. And
this is what God indicated had been done for Abraham when
"He gave him the covenant of circumcision." Read Rom. 4:11;
2:25–29; Phil. 3:3. {143}

The Law Magnifies the Promise

The law, as already seen, is not against the promise, because
it is in the promise. The promise that Abraham and his seed
should inherit the world, was "through the righteousness of
faith." But the law is righteousness, as God says: "Harken unto
Me, ye that know righteousness, the people in whose heart is
My law." Is. 51:7. So, then, the righteousness which the law
demands is the only righteousness that can inherit the promised
land, but it is obtained, not by the works of the law, but by faith.
The righteousness of the law is not attained by human efforts to
do the law, but by faith. See Rom. 9:30–32. Therefore, the
greater the righteousness which the law demands, the greater
is seen to be the promise of God; for He has promised to give it
to all who believe. Yea, He has sworn it. When, therefore, the
law was spoken from Sinai, "out of the midst of the fire, of the
cloud, and of the thick darkness, with a great voice," accompanied by the sounding of the trump of God, and with the whole
earth quaking at the presence of the Lord and all His holy
angels, thus indicating the inconceivable greatness and majesty
of the law of God, it was, to every one who remembered the oath
of God, but a revelation of the wondrous greatness of God's
promise; for all the righteousness which the law demands, He
has sworn to give to every one who trusts Him. The "loud voice"
with which the law was spoken, was the loud voice that from
the mountain-tops proclaims the glad tidings of the saving
mercy of God. See Is. 40:9. God's precepts are promises; they
{144} must necessarily be such, because He knows that men
have no power. All that God requires is what He gives. When
He says, "Thou shalt not," we may take it as His assurance that
if we but trust Him He will preserve us from the sin against
which He warns us. He will keep us from falling.

Conviction of Sin and of Righteousness

Jesus said of the Comforter, "When He is come, He will
reprove the world of sin, and of righteousness, and of judgment." n 16:8. Of Himself He said, "I came not to call the
righteous, but sinners to repentance." Mark 2:17. "They that are
whole have no need of the physician, but they that are sick." A
man must feel his need before he will accept help; he must know
his disease before he can apply the remedy. Even so the promise
of righteousness will be utterly unheeded by one who does not

realize that he is a sinner. The first part of the comforting work of the Holy Spirit, therefore, is to convince men of sin. So "the Scripture hath concluded all under sin, that the promise by faith of Jesus Christ might be given to them that believe." "By the law is the knowledge of sin." Rom. 3:20. He who knows that he is a sinner is in the way to acknowledge it; and "if we confess our sins, He is faithful and just to forgive us our sins, and to cleanse us from all unrighteousness." 1 . 1:9. Thus the law is in the hands of the Spirit an active agent in inducing men to accept the fullness of the promise. No one hates the man who has saved his life by pointing out to him an unknown peril; on the contrary, such an one is regarded as a {145} friend, and is always remembered with gratitude. Even so will the law be regarded by the one who has been prompted by its warning voice to flee from the wrath to come. He will ever say, with the psalmist, "I hate vain thoughts, but Thy law do I love."

Righteousness and Life

"If there had been a law given which could make alive, verily righteousness would have been of the law." This shows us that righteousness is life. It is no mere formula, no dead theory or dogma, but is living action. Christ is the life, and He is, therefore, our righteousness. "The Spirit is life because of righteousness." The law written on two tables of stone, could not give life, any more than could the stones on which it was written. All its precepts are perfect, but the flinty characters can not transform themselves into action. He who receives only the law in letter, has a "ministration of condemnation," and death. But "the Word was made flesh." In Christ, the Living Stone, the law is life and peace. Receiving Him through the "ministration of the Spirit," we have the life of righteousness, which the law approves.

This twenty-first verse shows that the giving of the law was to emphasize the importance of the promise. All the circumstances attending the giving of the law,—the trumpet tone, the awful voice, the quaking earth, the "fire, and blackness, and tempest," the thunders and lightnings, the bounds about the mount, beyond which it was death to pass,—all these told that "the law worketh wrath" to "the children of disobedience." But the very fact that the wrath {146} which the law works comes only on the children of disobedience, proves that the law is good, and that "the man that doeth them shall live in them." Did God wish to discourage the people?—Not by any means. The law must be kept, and the terrors of Sinai were designed to drive them back to the oath of God, which four hundred and thirty years before had been given to stand to all people in all ages as the assurance of righteousness through the crucified and ever-living Saviour.

All Shut Up in Prison

Note the similarity between verses 8 and 22. "The Scripture hath concluded [that is, shut up] all under sin, that the promise by faith of Jesus Christ might be given to them that believe." "The Scripture, foreseeing that God would justify the heathen through faith, preached before the Gospel unto Abraham, saying, In thee shall all nations be blessed." We see that the Gospel is preached by the same thing—the Scripture—that shuts men up under sin. The word "conclude" means literally "shut up," just as is given in verse 23. Of course, a person who is shut up by the law is in prison. In human governments a criminal is shut up as soon as the law can get hold of him; God's law is everywhere present, and always active, and, therefore, the instant a man sins he is shut up. This is the condition of all the world, "for all have sinned," and "there is none righteous, no, not one."

Those disobedient ones to whom Christ preached in the days of Noah were "in prison." 1 Pet. 3:19,20. But they, like all other sinners, were "prisoners {147} of hope." Zech. 9:12. God "hath looked down from the height of His sanctuary; from heaven did the Lord behold the earth; to hear the groaning of the prisoner; to loose those that are appointed to death." Ps. 102:19,20. Christ is given "for a covenant of the people, for a light of the Gentiles; to open the blind eyes, to bring out the prisoners from the prison, and them that sit in darkness out of the prison house." Is. 42:6,7.

Let me speak from personal experience to the sinner who does not yet know the joy and freedom of the Lord. Some day, if not already, you will be sharply convicted of sin by the Spirit of God. You may have been full of doubts and quibbles, of ready answers and self-defense, but then you will have nothing to say. You will then have no doubt about the reality of God and the Holy Spirit, and will need no argument to assure you of it; for you will know the voice of God speaking to your soul, and will feel, as did ancient Israel, "Let not God speak with us, lest we die." Then you will know what it is to be shut up in prison,—in a prison whose walls seem to close on you, not only barring all escape, but seeming to suffocate you. The tales of people condemned to be buried alive with a heavy stone upon them, will seem very vivid and real to you, as you feel the tables of the law crushing out your life, and a hand of marble seems to be breaking your very heart. Then it will give you joy to remember that you are shut up for the sole purpose that "the promise by faith of Jesus Christ" might be accepted by you. As soon as you lay hold of that promise,—the key that {148} will unlock any door in Doubting Castle,—the prison doors will fly open, and you can say, "Our soul is escaped as a bird out of the snare of the fowlers; the snare is broken, and we are escaped." Ps. 124:7.

Under the Law, Under Sin

We have just read that the Scripture hath shut up all under sin, that the promise by faith of Jesus Christ might be given to them that believe. Before faith came, we were kept in ward under the law, shut up unto the faith which should afterwards be revealed. We know that whatsoever is not of faith is sin (Rom. 14:23); therefore, to be under the law is identical with being under sin. We are under the law solely because we are under sin. The grace of God brings salvation from sin, so that when we accept God's grace we are no longer under the law, because we are freed from sin. Those who are under the law, therefore, are the transgressors of the law. The righteous are not under it, but are walking in it.

The Law a Jailer, a Taskmaster

"So that the law hath been our tutor unto Christ, that we might be justified by faith." The words "to bring us" are marked both in the old version and the new as having been added to the text, so we have dropped them out. It really makes no material difference with the sense whether they are retained or omitted. It will be noticed also that the new version has "tutor" in the place of "schoolmaster." This is better, but the sense is still better conveyed by the word that is used in the German and Scandinavian translations, which signifies "master of a house of correction." The {149} single word in our language corresponding to it would be jailer. The Greek word is the word which we have in English as "pedagogue." The paidagogos was the slave who accompanied the boys to school to see that they did not play truant. If they attempted to run away, he would bring them back, and had authority even to beat them to keep them in the way. The word has come to be used as meaning "schoolmaster," although the Greek word has not at all the idea of a schoolmaster. "Taskmaster" would be better. The idea here is rather that of a guard who accompanies a prisoner who is allowed to walk about outside the prison walls. The prisoner, although nominally at large, is really deprived of his liberty just the same as though he were actually in a cell. The fact is that all who do not believe are "under sin," "shut up" "under the law," and that, therefore, the law acts as their jailer. It is that that shuts them in, and will not let them off; the guilty can not escape in their guilt. God is merciful and gracious, but He will not clear the guilty. Ex. 34:6,7. That is, He will not lie, by calling evil good; but He provides a way by which the guilty may lose their guilt. Then the law will no longer be against them, will no longer shut them up, and they can walk at liberty.

Only One Door

Christ says, "I am the door." n 10:7,9. He is also the sheepfold and the Shepherd. Men fancy that when they are outside the fold they are free, and that to come into the fold would mean a curtailing of their liberty; but it is exactly the reverse. The fold of Christ is "a large place," while unbelief is a narrow {150} prison. The sinner can have but a narrow range of thought; the true "free thinker" is the one who comprehends with all saints what is the length, and breadth, and depth, and height of the love of Christ, which passeth knowledge. Outside of Christ is bondage; in Him alone is there freedom. Outside of Christ, the man is in prison, "holden with the cords of his sins." Prov. 5:22. "The strength of sin is the law." It is the law that declares him to be a sinner, and makes him conscious of his condition. "By the law is the knowledge of sin;" and "sin is not imputed when there is no law." Rom. 3:20; 5:13. The law really forms the sinner's prison walls. They close in on him, making him feel uncomfortable, oppressing him with a sense of sin, as though they would press his life out. In vain he makes frantic efforts to escape. Those commandments stand as firm as the everlasting hills. Whichever way he turns he finds a commandment which says to him, "You can find no freedom by me, for you have sinned." If he seeks to make friends with the law, and promises to keep it, he is no better off, for his sin still remains. It goads him and drives him to the only way of escape—"the promise by faith of Jesus Christ." In Christ he is made "free indeed," for in Christ he is made the righteousness of God. In Christ is "the perfect law of liberty."

The Law Preaches the Gospel

"But," says one, "the law says nothing of Christ." No; but all creation does speak of Christ, proclaiming the power of His salvation. We have seen that the cross of Christ, "Christ and Him {151} crucified," is to be seen in every leaf of the forest, and, indeed, in everything that exists. Not only so, but every fiber of man's being cries out for Christ. Men do not realize it, but Christ is "the Desire of all nations." It is He alone that "satisfies the desire of every living thing." Only in Him can relief be found for the world's unrest and longing. Now since Christ, in whom is peace, "for He is our peace," is seeking the weary and heavy-laden, and calling them to Himself, and every man has longings that nothing else in the world can satisfy, it is evident that if the man is awakened by the law to keener consciousness of his condition, and the law continues goading him, giving him no rest, and shutting up every other way of escape, the man must at last find the Door of Safety, for it always stands open. He is the City of Refuge, to which every one pursued by the avenger of blood may flee, sure of finding a welcome. In Christ alone will the sinner find release from the lash of the law, for in Christ the righteousness of the law is fulfilled, and by Him it is fulfilled in us. Rom. 8:4. The law is so far from requiring men to keep it in order to be saved, as some suppose, that it will not allow anybody to be saved unless he has "the righteousness which is of God by faith,"—the faith of Jesus Christ.

When Faith Is Come

Strangely enough, many have supposed that there was a definite time fixed for faith to come. This passage has been "interpreted" to mean that men were under the law until a certain time in the history of the world, and that at that time faith came, {152} and then they were henceforth free from the law. The coming of faith they make synonymous with the manifestation of Christ on earth. We can not say that anybody ever thought so, for such an "interpretation" indicates utter absence of thought about the matter. It would make men to be saved in bulk, regardless of any concurrence on their part. It would have it that up to a certain time all were in bondage under the law, and that from that time henceforth all were free from sin. A man's salvation would, therefore, depend simply on the accident of birth. If he lived before a certain time, he would be lost; if after, he would be saved. Such an absurdity need not take more of our time than the statement of it. No one can seriously think of the idea that the apostle is here speaking of a fixed, definite point of time in the history of the world, dividing between two so-called "dispensations," without at once abandoning it.

When, then, does faith come? "Faith cometh by hearing, and hearing by the Word of God." Rom. 10:17. Whenever a man receives the Word of God, the word of promise, which brings with it the fullness of the law, and no longer fights against it, but yields to it, then faith comes to him. Read the eleventh chapter of Hebrews, and you will see that faith came from the beginning. Since the days of Abel, men have found freedom by faith. The only time fixed is "now," "to-day." "Now is the accepted time; behold, now is the day of salvation." "To-day if ye will hear His voice, harden not your hearts." {153}

Putting on Christ by Baptism

"As many of you as have been baptized into Christ have put on Christ." "Know ye not, that so many of us as were baptized into Jesus Christ were baptized into His death?" Rom. 6:3. It is by His death that Christ redeems us from the curse of the law; but we must die with Him. Baptism is "the likeness of His death." We rise to walk "in newness of life," even Christ's life.

See Gal. 2:20. Having put on Christ, we are one in Him. We are completely identified with Him. Our identity is lost in His. It is often said of one who has been converted, "He is so changed you would not know him; he is not the same man." No, he is not. God has turned him into "another man." Therefore, being one with Christ, he has a right to whatever Christ has, and a right to "the heavenly places" where Christ sits. From the prison house of sin, he is exalted to the dwelling-place of God. This, of course, presupposes that baptism is with him a reality, not a mere outward form. It is not simply into the visible water that he is baptized, but "into Christ," into His life.

Baptism Doth Save Us

The word "baptism," which is the Greek word transferred, not translated, has but one meaning, namely, to plunge into, to dip, to immerse. The Greek blacksmith baptized his iron in the water, to cool it. The housewife baptized her dishes in water, in order to clean them; and for the same purpose all would baptize their hands in water. yea, every man would baptize himself frequently, going {154} to the baptisterion, that is, the immersing pool, for that purpose. We have the same word transferred as "baptistery." It was and is a place where people could plunge in, and be wholly immersed in water.

That is not being "baptized into Christ," but it indicates what must be our relation to Him when we are baptized into Him. We must be swallowed up and lost to sight in His life. Only Christ will henceforth be seen, so that "it is no more I, but Christ," for "we are buried with Him by baptism into death." Rom. 6:4. baptism doth save us "by the resurrection of Jesus Christ" from the dead (1 Pet. 3:21), because we are "baptized into His death," that "like as Christ was raised up from the dead by the glory of the Father, even so we also should walk in newness of life." Being reconciled to God by the death of Christ, we are "saved by His life." Rom. 5:10. So baptism into Christ, not the mere form, but the fact, does save us.

This baptism is "the answer of a good conscience toward God." If there be not a good conscience toward God, there is no Christian baptism. Therefore, the person to be baptized must be old enough to have a conscience in the matter. He must have a consciousness of sin, and also of forgiveness by Christ. He must know the life that is manifested, and must willingly give up his old life of sin for the new life of righteousness.

Baptism is "not the putting away of the filth of the flesh" (1 Pet. 3:21), not the outward cleansing of the body, but the purging of the soul and conscience. There is a fountain opened for sin and for uncleanness {155} (Zech. 13:1), and this fountain is the blood, the life of Christ. That life flows in a stream from the throne of God, in the midst of which is the slain Lamb (Rev. 5:6), even as it flowed from the side of Christ on the cross. When, "through the eternal Spirit," He had offered Himself to God, there flowed from His side blood and water (n 19:34), "for there are three who bear witness, the Spirit, and the water, and the blood; and the three agree in one" (1 . 5:8, R.V.). All these are also one with the Word, which is Spirit and life. n 6:63. Christ "loved the church, and gave Himself for it; that He might sanctify and cleanse it with the washing of water by the Word." Eph. 5:25,26. Literally, "a water bath in the Word." In being buried in the water, in the name of the Father, Son, and Holy Spirit, the conscientious believer signifies his acceptance of the water of life, the blood of Christ, which cleanses from all sin, and that he gives himself to live henceforth by every word that proceeds out of the mouth of God. From that time he disappears from sight, and only the life of Christ is manifested in his mortal flesh.

One in Christ, the Seed

"There is neither Jew nor Greek, there is neither bond nor free, there is neither male nor female; for ye are all one in Christ Jesus." "There is no difference." This is the key-note of the Gospel. All are alike sinners, and all are saved in the same way. They who would make a distinction on the ground of nationality, claiming that there is something different for the Jew than for the Gentile, might just as {156} well make a difference on the ground of sex, claiming that women can not be saved in the same way and at the same time as men, or that a servant can not be saved in the same way as his master. No; there is but one way, and all human beings, of whatever race or condition, are equal before God. "Ye are all one in Christ Jesus," and Christ is the One. So it is that "He saith not, And to seeds, as of many; but as of one, And to thy Seed, which is Christ." "For ye are all one in Christ Jesus. And if ye be Christ's, then are ye Abraham's seed, and heirs according to the promise." There is but one seed, but it embraces all who are Christ's.

Only One Man

In putting on Christ, we "put on the new man, which after God is created in righteousness and true holiness." Eph. 4:24. He has abolished in His flesh the enmity,—the carnal mind,—"for to make in Himself of twain one new man." Eph. 2:15. He alone is the real man,—"the Man Christ Jesus." Outside of Him there is no real manhood. We come unto "a perfect man" only when we arrive at "the measure of the stature of the fullness of Christ." Eph. 4:13. In the fullness of time God will gather together in one all things in Christ. There will be but one Man, and only one Man's righteousness, even as the secd is but one.

But "if ye be Christ's, then are ye Abraham's seed, and heirs according to the promise."

"Until the Seed Should Come"

It needs not many words now to determine what is meant by the phrase, "till the seed should come to whom the promise was made." {157}

We know what the seed is,—all who are Christ's,—and we know that it has not yet come in its fullness. To be sure, Christ was once manifested on earth in the flesh, but He did not receive the promised inheritance, any more than Abraham did. Abraham had not so much as to put his foot on (Acts 7:5), and Christ had not where to lay His head. Moreover, Christ can not come into the inheritance until Abraham does also, for the promise was "to Abraham and to his seed." The Lord by the prophet Ezekiel spoke of the inheritance at the time when David ceased to have a representative on his throne on earth, and He foretold the overthrow of Babylon, Persia, Greece, and Rome, in these words: "Remove the diadem, and take off the crown; this shall not be the same; exalt him that is low, and abase him that is high. I will overturn, overturn, overturn it; and it shall be no more, until He come whose right it is; and I will give it Him." Eze. 21:26,27.

So Christ sits on His Father's throne, "from henceforth expecting till His enemies be made His footstool." Soon will He come, but not until the last soul has accepted Him that can by any possibility be induced to accept salvation. Those who are led by the Spirit of God, are the sons of God, and joint-heirs with Christ, so that Christ can not come into the inheritance before they do. The seed is one, not divided. When He comes to execute judgment, and to slay those who said, "We will not have this Man to reign over us," He comes "with ten thousands of His holy ones." Jude 14.

Then will the seed be complete, and the promise will be fulfilled. And until that time the law will {158} faithfully perform its task of stirring up and pricking the consciences of sinners, giving them no rest until they become identified with Christ, or cast Him off altogether. Do you accept the terms? Will you cease your complaints against the law which would save you from sinking into a fatal sleep? And will you in Christ accept its righteousness? Then, as Abraham's seed, and an heir according to the promise, you can rejoice in your freedom from the bondage of sin, singing:—

"I'm the child of a King,
The child of a King,
With Jesus my Saviour,
I'm the child of a King." {159}

The Adoption Of Sons

A Little Retrospect

IT is absolutely impossible to exhaust any portion of Scripture. The more one studies it, the more one sees in it, and not only that, but the more one becomes conscious of the fact that there is much more in it than appears to view. The Word of God, like Himself, is absolutely unfathomable. One's understanding of any given portion of the Scripture depends on the thoroughness of his knowledge of that which precedes it. Let us, therefore, give a little further attention to that portion of the third chapter of this Epistle which treats of

The Seed

First of all, it must be borne in mind that Christ is the Seed. That is plainly stated. But Christ did not live for Himself, and He is not heir simply for Himself. He has won an inheritance, not for Himself, but for His brethren. God's purpose is to "gather together in one all things in Christ." He will finally put an end to divisions of every kind, and He does it now in those who accept Him. In Christ there are no distinctions of nationality, and no classes and ranks. No Christian thinks of any other man as English, German, French, Russian, Turk, Chinese, {160} or African, but simply as a man, and, therefore, a possible heir of God through Christ. If that other man, no matter what his race or nation, be also a Christian, then the bond becomes mutual, and, therefore, still stronger. "There is neither Jew nor Greek, there is neither bond nor free, there is neither male nor female; for ye are all one in Christ Jesus." It is for this reason that it is impossible for a Christian to engage in war. He knows no distinction of nationality, but regards all men as his brothers. But the chief reason why he can not engage in warfare is that the life of Christ is his life, for he is one with Christ; and it would be as impossible for him to fight as it would be for Christ to seize a sword and wield it in self-defense; and two Christians can no more fight against each other than Christ can fight against Himself.

However, we are not now engaged in discussing war, but are merely showing the absolute unity of believers in Christ. They are one. There is, therefore, but one Seed, and that is Christ; for, however many millions of true believers there may be, they are only one in Christ. Each man has his own individuality, but it is in every case only the manifestation of some phase of the individuality of Christ. In a human body there are many members, and all members have not the same office, but differ in their individuality; yet there is absolute unity and harmony in every healthy body. With those who have put on the new man, which is renewed in knowledge after the image of Him that created him, "there is neither Greek nor Jew, circumcision nor uncircumcision, {161} Barbarian, Scythian, bond nor free; but Christ is all, and in all." Col. 3:11.

The Harvest

In Christ's explanation of the parable of the tares and the wheat, we are told that "the good seed are the children of the kingdom." Matt. 13:38. The man would not allow the tares to be pulled out of the wheat, because in the early stage it would be difficult to distinguish in every case between the wheat and the tares, and some of the wheat would be destroyed. So he said, "Let both grow together until the harvest; and in the time of harvest I will say to the reapers, Gather ye together first the tares, and bind them in bundles to burn them; but gather the wheat into my barn." It is in the harvest that the seed is gathered. Everybody knows that. But what the parable especially shows is that it is in the harvest that the seed is fully manifested; in short, that the seed comes at harvest time. The harvest only waits for the seed to be fully manifested and matured. But "the harvest is the end of the world." So the time when "the seed should come to whom the promise was made," is the end of the world, when the time comes for the promise of the new earth to be fulfilled. Indeed, the seed can not possibly be said to come before that time, since the end of the world will come just as soon as the last person who can be induced to accept Christ has done so; and the seed is not complete as long as there is one grain lacking. {162}

Read now, in the nineteenth verse of the third chapter, that the law was spoken because of transgression, "till the seed should come to whom the promise was made." What do we learn from that?—Simply this, that the law as spoken from Sinai, without the change of a single letter, is an integral part of the Gospel, and must be presented in the Gospel until the second coming of Christ, at the end of the world. "Till heaven and earth pass, one jot or one tittle shall in nowise pass from the law." And what of the time when heaven and earth pass, and the new heaven and the new earth come?—Then the law will not be needed written in a book, for men to preach to sinners, showing them their sins, for it will be in the heart of every man. Heb. 8:10,11. Done away?—Not by any means; but indelibly engraved in the heart of every individual, written not with ink, but with the Spirit of the living God.

With the truth concerning the seed before us, and the parable of the wheat and the tares fresh in our minds, let us proceed in our study.

"But I say that so long as the heir is a child, he differeth nothing from a bond-servant, though he is lord of all; but is under guardians and stewards until the term appointed of the father. So we also, when we were children, were held in bondage under the rudiments of the world; but when the fullness of the time came, God sent forth His Son, born of a woman, born under the law, that He might redeem them which were under the law, that we might receive the adoption of sons. And because ye are sons, God sent forth the Spirit of His Son into our hearts, crying, {163} Abba, Father. So that thou art no longer a bond-servant, but a son; and if a son, then an heir through God.

"Howbeit at that time, not knowing God, ye were in bondage to them which by nature are no gods; but now that ye have come to know God, or rather to be known of God, how turn ye back again to the weak and beggarly rudiments, whereunto ye desire to be in bondage over again? Ye observe days, and months, and seasons, and years. I am afraid of you, lest by any means I have bestowed labor upon you in vain.

"I beseech you, brethren, be as I am, for I am as ye are. Ye did me no wrong; but ye know that because of an infirmity of the flesh I preached the Gospel unto you the first time; and that which was a temptation to you in my flesh ye despised not, nor rejected; but ye received me as an angel of God, even as Christ Jesus. Where then is that gratulation of yourselves? for I bear you witness, that, if possible, ye would have plucked out your eyes and given them to me. So then am I become your enemy, because I tell you the truth? They zealously seek you in no good way; nay, they desire to shut you out, that ye may seek them. But it is good to be zealously sought in a good matter at all times, and not only when I am present with you. My little children, of whom I am again in travail until Christ be formed in you, yea, I could wish to be present with you now, and to change my voice; for I am perplexed about you.

"Tell me, ye that desire to be under the law, do ye {164} not hear the law? For it is written, that Abraham had two sons, one by the handmaid, and one by the freewoman. Howbeit the son by the handmaid is born after the flesh; but the son by the freewoman is born through promise. Which things contain an allegory; for these women are two covenants; one from Mount Sinai, bearing children unto bondage, which is Hagar. Now this Hagar is Mount Sinai in Arabia, and answereth to the Jerusalem that now is; for she is in bondage with her children. But the

Jerusalem that is above is free, which is our mother. For it is written:—

"Rejoice, thou barren that bearest not;
Break forth and cry, thou that travailest not;
For more are the children of the desolate
than of her which hath the husband.
Now we, brethren, as Isaac was, are children of
promise. But as then he that was born after the flesh
persecuted him that was born after the Spirit, even so
it is now. Howbeit what saith the Scripture? Cast out
the handmaid and her son; for the son of the
handmaid shall not inherit with the son of the
freewoman. Wherefore, brethren, we are not children
of a handmaid, but of a freewoman." Galatians 4,
R.V.

A Statement of Fact

It must be apparent to all that the chapter division makes no difference in the subject. The third chapter closes with a statement as to who are heirs, and the fourth chapter proceeds with a study of the question of heirship. The first two verses explain {165} themselves. They are a simple statement of fact. Although a child may be heir to a vast estate, he has no more to do with it until he is of age, than a servant has. If he should never come of age, then he would never actually enter upon his inheritance. He would have lived all his life as a servant, so far as any share in the inheritance is concerned. Now for

The Application

"So we also, when we were children, were held in bondage under the rudiments of the world." If we look ahead to the fifth verse, we shall see that the state here known as "children" is that before we receive "the adoption of sons." It represents the condition before we were redeemed from the curse of the law, that is, before we were converted. It does not, therefore, mean children of God, as distinguished from worldlings, but the "children" of whom the apostle speaks in Eph. 4:14, "tossed to and fro, and carried about with every wind of doctrine, by the sleight of men, and cunning craftiness, whereby they lie in wait to deceive." In short, it refers to us in our unconverted state, when we "were by nature the children of wrath, even as others."

The Rudiments of the World

"When we were children," we were in bondage under the rudiments of the world. No one who has the slightest acquaintance with the Lord needs to be told that the rudiments of the world have nothing in common with Him, and do not proceed from Him. "For all that is in the world, {166} the lust of the flesh, and the lust of the eyes, and the pride of life, is not of the Father, but is of the world. And the world passeth away, and the lust thereof." 1 . 2:16,17. The friendship of the world is enmity with God. "Whosoever therefore will be a friend of the world is the enemy of God." Jam. 4:4. It is from "this present evil world" that Christ came to deliver us. We are warned to "take heed lest there shall be any one that maketh spoil of you through his philosophy and vain deceit, after the tradition of men, after the rudiments of the world, and not after Christ." Col. 2:8. The bondage to the rudiments of the world is the condition of walking "according to the course of this world," "in the lusts of our flesh, fulfilling the desires of the flesh and of the mind;" being "by nature the children of wrath." Eph. 2:1–3. It is the same bondage that is described in Gal. 3:22–24, before faith came, when we were under the law, "under sin." It is the condition of men who are "without Christ, being aliens from the commonwealth of Israel, and strangers from the covenants of promise, having no hope, and without God in the world." Eph. 2:12.

All Men Possible Heirs

It may be asked, If such is the condition of those here referred to as "children," how can they be spoken of as heirs? The answer is plain. It is on the principle that it is not manifest who constitute the seed, until the harvest. God has not cast off the human race; therefore, since the first man created was called "the son of God," it follows that all men are heirs in the sense that they are in their minority. {167}

As already learned, "before faith came," although all were wanderers from God, we were kept under the law, guarded by a severe master, "shut up," in order that we might be led to accept the promise. What a blessed thing it is that God counts even the ungodly, those who are in the bondage of sin, as His children,—wandering, prodigal sons, but still children. God has made all men "accepted in the Beloved." This probationary life is given us for the purpose of giving us a chance to acknowledge Him as Father, and to become sons indeed. But, unless we come back to Him, we shall die as slaves of sin.

"The Fullness of the Time"

Christ came in the fullness of time. A parallel statement to this is found in Rom. 5:6: "When we were yet without strength, in due time Christ died for the ungodly." But the death of Christ serves for those who live now and for those who lived before He was manifested in the flesh in Judea, just as well as for the men who lived at that time. His death made no more change eighteen hundred years ago than it did four thousand years ago. It had no more effect on the men of that generation than on the men of any other generation. It is once for all, and, therefore, has an equal effect on every age. "The fullness of time" was the time foretold in prophecy, when the Messiah should be revealed; but the redemption was for all men in all ages. He was foreordained before the foundation of the world, but was "manifest in these last times." 1 Pet. 1:20. If it had been God's plan that He should have been revealed in this century, or even not until the last year {168} before the close of time, it would have made no difference with the Gospel. "He ever liveth," and He ever has lived, "the same yesterday, and to-day, and forever." It is "through the eternal Spirit" that He offers Himself for us (Heb. 9:14), so that the sacrifice is equally present and efficacious in every age.

"Born of a Woman"

God sent forth His Son, born of a woman, and, therefore, a veritable man. He lived an average lifetime on this earth in the flesh, and suffered all the ills and troubles that fall to the lot of "man that is born of woman." "The Word was made flesh." Christ always designated Himself as "the Son of man," thus forever identifying Himself with the whole human race. The bond of union can never be broken.

"Born under the Law"

Being born of a woman, Christ was necessarily born under the law, for such is the condition of all mankind, and "in all things it behooved Him to be made like unto His brethren, that He might be a merciful and faithful High Priest in things pertaining to God, to make reconciliation for the sins of the people." Heb. 2:17. He takes everything on Himself. "He hath borne our griefs, and carried our sorrows." "Himself took our infirmities, and bare our disease." Matt. 8:17, R.V. "All we like sheep have gone astray; we have turned every one to his own way; and the Lord hath laid on Him the iniquity of us all." He redeems us by coming into our place literally, and taking our load off our shoulders. "Him who knew no sin He made to be sin on our {169} behalf; that we might become the righteousness of God in Him." 2 Cor. 5:21, R.V. In the fullest sense of the word, and to a degree that is seldom thought of when the expression is used, He became man's substitute. That is, He permeates our being, identifying Himself so fully with us that everything that touches or affects us touches and affects Him. He is not our substitute in the sense that one man is a substitute for another, in the army, for instance, the substitute being in one place, while the one for whom he is substitute is somewhere else, engaged in some other service. No; Christ's substitution is far different. He is our substitute in that He substitutes Himself for us, and we appear no more. We drop out entirely, so that it is "not I, but Christ." Thus we cast our cares on Him, not by picking them up and with an effort throwing them on Him, but by humbling ourselves into the nothingness that we are, so that we leave the burden resting on Him alone. Thus we see already how it is that He came "To Redeem Them That Were under the Law."

He does it in the most practical and real way. Whom does He redeem?—"Them that were under the law." We can not refrain from referring for a moment to the idea that some have that this expression, "to redeem them that were under the law," has a mere local application. They would have it that it means that Christ freed the Jews from the necessity of offering sacrifices, or from any further obligation to keep the commandments. Well, suppose we take it as referring only to the Jews, and especially to {170} those who lived at the time of His first advent; what then?—Simply this, that we shut ourselves off from any place in the plan of redemption. If it was only the Jews that were under the law, then it was only the Jews that Christ came to redeem. Ah, we do not like to be left out, when it comes to the matter of redemption! Then we must acknowledge that we are, or were before we believed, "under the law;" for Christ came to redeem none but those who were under the law. "Under the law," as we have already seen, means condemned by the law as transgressors. Christ did "not come to call the righteous, but sinners to repentance." But the law condemns none but those who are amenable to it, and who ought to keep it. Therefore, since Christ redeems us from the law, from its condemnation, it follows that He redeems us to a life of obedience to it.

"That We Might Receive the Adoption of Sons"

"Beloved, now are we the sons of God." 1 . 3:2. "As many as received Him, to them gave He power to become the sons of God, even to them that believe on His name." n 1:12. This is an altogether different state from that described in the third verse as "children." In that state we were "a rebellious people, lying children, children that will not hear the law of the Lord." Is. 30:9. Believing on Jesus, and receiving the adoption of sons, we are described "as obedient children, not fashioning yourselves according to the former lusts in your ignorance." 1 Pet. 1:14. Christ said, "I delight to do Thy will, O My God; yea, Thy law is within My {171} heart." Ps. 40:8. Therefore, since He becomes our substitute, as described in the last paragraph but one, literally taking our place, not instead of us, but coming into us, and living our life in us and for us, it necessarily follows that the same law must be within our hearts when we receive the adoption of sons.

The Witness of the Spirit

"It is the Spirit that beareth witness, because the Spirit is truth." 1 . 5:6. "Because ye are sons, God hath sent forth the Spirit of His Son into your hearts, crying, Abba, Father," or, Father, Father. Oh, what joy and peace come with the entering of the Spirit into the heart as a permanent resident; not as a guest merely, but as sole proprietor! Being justified by faith we have peace with God through our Lord Jesus Christ, so that we "joy in God," rejoicing even in tribulations, having hope that never disappoints, because "the love of God is shed abroad in our hearts by the Holy Ghost which is given unto us." Rom. 5:1–5. Then we can love even as God does; we have the same love, because we have the Divine nature. "The Spirit itself beareth witness with our spirit, that we are the children of God." "He that believeth hath the witness in himself."

"No More a Servant, but a Son"

"Thou art no more a servant, but a son." It will be seen that as there are two kinds of children, so there are two classes of servants. In the first part of this chapter we have the word "children" used to designate those who are not "of full {172} age," and have not their senses exercised to discern both good and evil. Heb. 5:14. The promise is to them, even as it is "to all that are afar off," but it remains to be seen if they will, by accepting it, become partakers of the divine nature, and so sons of God indeed. While thus the children of wrath, men are servants of sin, not servants of God. The Son of God is a servant, but a servant in a far different sense from the servant here referred to. The character of the servant depends on the master whom he serves. In this chapter the word "servant" invariably applies, not to servants of God, who are really sons, but to the bond-servants of sin. Between such a servant and a son there is a vast difference. The slave can not possess anything; he has no control over himself, and this is his distinguishing characteristic. The free-born son, on the contrary, has dominion over every created thing, as in the beginning, because he has the victory over himself; for "he that is slow to anger is better than the mighty; and he that ruleth his spirit than he that taketh a city."

"If a Son, Then an Heir"

When the prodigal son was wandering from the father's house, he differed nothing from a servant, because he was a servant, doing the most menial drudgery. In that condition he came back to the old homestead, feeling that he deserved no better place than that of a servant. But the father saw him while he was yet a long way off, and ran and met him, and received him as a son, and, therefore, as an heir, although he had forfeited all right {173} to heirship. So we have forfeited our right to be called sons, and have squandered away the inheritance; yet God receives us in Christ as sons indeed, and gives us the same rights and privileges that Christ has. Although Christ is now in heaven at the right hand of God, "far above all principality, and power, and might, and dominion, and every name that is named, not only in this world, but also in that which is to come" (Eph. 1:20,21), He has nothing that He does not share with us; for "God, who is rich in mercy, for His great love wherewith He loved us, even when we were dead in sins, hath quickened [made alive] us together with Christ, and hath raised us up together, and made us sit together in heavenly places in Christ" (Eph. 2:4–6). Christ is one with us in our present suffering, that we may be one with Him in His present glory. He "hath exalted them of low degree." Even now "He raiseth up the poor out of the dust, and lifteth up the beggar from the dunghill, to set them among princes, and to make them inherit the throne of glory." 1 Sam. 2:8. No king on earth has so great possessions, nor so much actual power, as the poorest peasant who knows the Lord as his Father.

Heathen Bondage

The apostle Paul, writing to the Corinthians, said, "Ye know that ye were Gentiles, carried away unto these dumb idols, even as ye were led." 1 Cor. 12:2. Even so it was with the Galatians. To them he wrote, "Not knowing God, ye were in bondage to them which by nature are no gods." If this fact is {174} borne in mind, it will save the reader from falling into some very common errors in opinion concerning this Epistle. The Galatians had been heathen, worshiping idols, and in bondage to the most degrading superstitions. Bear in mind that this bondage is the same as that which is spoken of in the preceding chapter,—they were "shut up" under the law. It was the very same bondage in which all unconverted persons are, for in the second and third chapters of Romans we are told that "there is no difference; for all have sinned." The Jews themselves, who did not know the Lord by personal experience, were in the same bondage,—the bondage of sin. "Every one that committeth sin is the bond-servant of sin." n 8:34, R.V. And "he that committeth sin is of the devil." 1 . 3:8. "The things which the Gentiles sacrifice, they sacrifice to devils, and not to God." 1 Cor. 10:20. If a man is not a Christian, he is a heathen; there is no middle ground. If the Christian apostatizes, he immediately becomes a heathen. We ourselves once walked "according to the course of this world, according to the prince of the power of the air, the spirit that now worketh in the children of disobedience" (Eph. 2:2), and we "were aforetime foolish, disobedient, deceived, serving divers lusts and pleasures, living in malice and envy, hateful, hating one another" (Titus 3:3, R.V.). So we also were "in bondage to them which by nature are no gods." The meaner the master, the worse the bondage. What language can depict the horror of being in bondage to corruption itself? {175}

In Love with Bondage

"Now that ye have come to know God, or rather to be known of God, how turn ye back again to the weak and beggarly rudiments, whereunto ye desire to be in bondage over again?" Is it not strange that men should be in love with chains? Christ has proclaimed "liberty to the captives, and the opening of the prison to them that are bound" (Is. 61:1), saying to the prisoners, "Go forth," and to them that are in darkness, "Show yourselves" (Is. 49:9); yet men who have heard these words, and have come forth, and have seen the light of "the Sun of Righteousness," and have tasted the sweets of liberty, actually turn round and go back into their prison, submit to be bound with their old chains, even fondling them, and labor away at the hard treadmill of sin. Who has not had something of that experience? It is no fancy picture. It is a fact that men can come to love the most revolting things, even death itself; for Wisdom says, "All they that hate Me love death." Prov. 8:36. In the Epistle to the Galatians we have a vivid picture of human experience.

Observing Heathen Customs

"Ye observe days, and months, and times, and years." This was an evidence of their bondage. "Ah," says some one, "they had gone back to the old Jewish Sabbath; that was the bondage against which Paul would warn us!" How strange it is that men have such an insane hatred of the Sabbath, which the Lord Himself gave to the Jews, in common with all other people on the earth, that they will seize upon every word that they think they can turn against it, {176} although in order to do so they must shut their eyes to all the words that are around it! Anybody who reads the Epistle to the Galatians, and thinks as he reads, must know that the Galatians were not Jews. They had been converted from heathenism. Therefore, previous to their conversion they had never had anything to do with any religious custom that was practiced by the Jews. They had nothing whatever in common with the Jews. Consequently, when they turned again to the "weak and beggarly elements" to which they were willing again to be in bondage, it is evident that they were not going back to any Jewish practice. They were going back to their old heathen customs. "But were not the men who were perverting them Jews?"—Yes, they were. But remember this one thing, when you seek to turn a man away from Christ to some substitute for Christ, you can not tell where he will end.

You can not make him stop just where you want him to. If a converted drunkard loses faith in Christ, he will take up his drinking habits as surely as he lives, even though the Lord may have taken the appetite away from him. So when these "false brethren"—Jewish opposers of "the truth of the Gospel" as it is in Christ—succeeded in seducing the Galatians from Christ, they could not get them to stop with Jewish ceremonies. No; they inevitably drifted back to their old heathen superstitions.

Forbidden Practices

Read the tenth verse again, and then read Deut. 18:10: "There shall not be found among you any one that maketh his son or his daughter to pass through {177} the fire, or that useth divination, or an observer of times, or an enchanter, or a witch." Now read what the Lord says to the heathen who would shield themselves from just judgment that is about to come upon them: "Thou art wearied in the multitude of thy counsels. Let now the astrologers, the star-gazers, the monthly prognosticators, stand up, and save thee from these things that shall come upon thee." Is. 47:13. Here we see that the very things to which the Galatians were returning, were forbidden by the Lord when He brought Israel out of Egypt. Now we might as well say that when God forbade these things He was warning the Israelites against keeping the Sabbath, as to say that Paul was upbraiding the Galatians for keeping it, or that he had any reference to it whatever. God forbade these things at the very time when He gave the commandment concerning Sabbath-keeping. So far back into their old ways had the Galatians gone that Paul was afraid lest all his labor on them had been in vain. They were forsaking God and returning to "the weak and beggarly elements of the world," which no reverent person can think of as ever having had any connection with God. They were changing their glory for "that which doth not profit" (Jer. 2:11); for "the customs of the heathen are vain."

There is just as much danger for us in this respect as there ever was for any people. Whoever trusts in himself, having any confidence whatever in the flesh, is worshiping the works of his own hands instead of God, just as truly as does any one who makes and bows down to a graven image. It is so easy for a {178} man to trust to his own supposed shrewdness, to his ability to "take care of himself," and to forget that the thoughts even of the wise are vain, and that there is no power but of God. "Let not the wise man glory in his wisdom, neither let the mighty man glory in his might, let not the rich man glory in his riches; but let him that glorieth glory in this, that he understandeth and knoweth Me, that I am the Lord which exercise loving-kindness, judgment, and righteousness, in the earth; for in these things I delight, saith the Lord." Jer. 9:23,24.

The Messenger Not Personally Affronted

"He whom God hath sent speaketh the words of God." n 3:34. The apostle Paul was sent by God and the Lord Jesus Christ, and did not speak his own words. He was a messenger, bearing a message from God, and not from any man. The work was not his, nor any other man's, but God's, and he was but the humble instrument, the earthen vessel, which God had chosen as the means of carrying His glorious Gospel of grace. Therefore, Paul did not feel affronted when his message was unheeded or even rejected. "Ye have not injured me at all," he says. He did not regret the labor that he had bestowed upon the Galatians, on his own account, as though it were so much of his time wasted; but he was fearful for them, lest his labor had been in vain as far as they were concerned. The man who from the heart can say, "Not unto us, O Lord, not unto us, but unto Thy name give glory, for Thy mercy, and for Thy truth's sake" (Ps. 115:1), can not feel personally injured {179} if his message is not received. Whoever becomes irritated or angry when his teaching is slighted or ignored or scornfully rejected, shows either that he has forgotten that it was God's words that he was speaking, or else that he had mingled with them or substituted for them words of his own. This is what has led to all the persecution that has disgraced the professed Christian church. Men have arisen speaking perverse things to draw away disciples after themselves, and when their sayings and customs were not heeded, they have been offended, and have visited their vengeance on the so-called heretics. No one in all the ages has ever suffered persecution for failure to obey the commandments of God, but only for neglect of human customs and traditions. It is a grand thing always to be zealous in a good thing, but let the zeal be according to sanctified knowledge. The zealous person should frequently ask himself, Whose servant am I? If he is God's servant, then he will be content with delivering the message that God has given him, leaving vengeance to God, to whom it belongs.

Power in Weakness

"Ye know that because of an infirmity of the flesh I preached the Gospel unto you the first time." From the incidental statements in this Epistle we can easily gather the history of the experience of the Galatian brethren, and of Paul's relation to it. Having been detained in Galatia by physical weakness, he preached the Gospel "in demonstration of the Spirit and of power," so that the people saw Christ crucified among them, and, accepting Him, were filled with {180} the power and joy of the Holy Ghost. Their joy and blessedness in the Lord was testified to publicly, and they suffered much persecution in consequence; but this they counted as nothing. Paul, in spite of his unsightly appearance (compare 1 Cor. 2:1–5; 2 Cor. 10:10), was received as God's own messenger, because of the joyful news that he brought. So highly did they appreciate the riches of grace which he had opened up to them, that they would gladly have given their own eyes to supply his deficiency. All this is referred to in order that the Galatians may see from what they have fallen, as they consider their present barrenness, and that they may know that the apostle was disinterested in his solicitude for them. He told them the truth once, and they rejoiced in it; it is not possible that he is become their enemy because he continues to tell them the same truth.

But there is still more in these personal references. We must not imagine that Paul was pleading for personal sympathy when he referred to his afflictions, and to the great inconvenience under which he had labored. Far from it. Not for a moment did he lose sight of the purpose for which he was writing, namely, to show that "the flesh profiteth nothing," but that everything of good is from the Holy Spirit of God. The Galatians had "begun in the Spirit." Paul was naturally small of stature, and weak in body, and was suffering special affliction when he first met them; yet, in spite of his almost absolute helplessness, he preached the Gospel with such mighty power that none could fail to see that there was a real, although unseen, presence with him. The {181} Gospel is not of man, but of God. It was not made known to them by the flesh, and they were not indebted to the flesh for any of the blessings that they had received. What blindness, what infatuation, then, for them to think to perfect by their own efforts that which nothing but the power of God could begin! Have we learned this lesson?

Where Is the Blessedness?

Everybody who has ever had any acquaintance with the Lord, knows that in accepting Him there is joy. It is always expected that a new convert will have a beaming countenance, and a joyful testimony. So it had been with the Galatians. But now their expressions of thanksgiving had given place to bickering and strife. See Gal. 5:15. Is it not strange that people do not expect that old Christians will have as much enthusiasm as young converts? that it is taken for granted that the first joy, and the warmth of the first love, will gradually die away? So it is, but so it should not be. That which God has against His people is this, that they have left their first love. Rev. 2:4. "The path of the just is as the shining light, that shineth more and more unto the perfect day." Prov. 4:18. Note that this is the path of the just, and the just are they who live by faith. When men turn from the faith, or attempt to substitute works for it, the light goes out. Jesus said, "These things have I spoken unto you, that My joy might remain in you, and that your joy might be full." n 15:11. He gives the oil of joy—the Holy Spirit—for mourning, and that is abiding. The life is manifested that we might have fullness {182} of joy. 1 . 1:1–4. The fountain of life is never exhausted; the supply is never diminished. If, therefore, our light grows dim, and our joy gives place to a dull, monotonous grind, we may know that we have turned aside out of the way of life.

Desiring to Be under the Law

"Tell me, ye that desire to be under the law, do ye not hear the law?" After what we have already had, there will be no one to come with the objection that to be under the law can not be a very deplorable condition, else the Galatians would not have desired to be under it. "There is a way that seemeth right unto a man; but the end thereof are the ways of death." Prov. 16:25. How many there are who love ways that everybody except themselves can see are leading them direct to death; yes, there are many who, with their eyes wide open to the consequences of their course, will persist in it, deliberately choosing "the pleasures of sin for a season," rather than righteousness and length of days. To be "under the law" of God is to be condemned by it as a sinner chained and doomed to death, yet many millions besides the Galatians have loved the condition, and still love it. Ah, if they would only hear what it says! There is no reason why they should not hear it, for it speaks in thunder tones. "He that hath ears to hear, let him hear."

"What Saith the Law?"

It saith, "Cast out the bondwoman and her son; for the son of the bondwoman shall not be heir with the son of the free-woman." It speaks death {183} to all who take pleasure in the beggarly elements of the world. "Cursed is every one that continueth not in all things which are written in the book of the law to do them." To what place shall the wicked bond-servant be cast out?—"Into outer darkness; there shall be weeping and gnashing of teeth." "For, behold, the day cometh, that shall burn as an oven; and all the proud, yea, and all that do wickedly, shall be stubble; and the day that cometh shall burn them up, saith the Lord of hosts, that it shall leave them neither root nor branch." Therefore, "Remember ye the law of Moses My servant, which I commanded unto him in Horeb for all Israel, with the statutes and judgments." Mal. 4:1,4. All who are under the law, whether they be called Jews or Gentiles, Christians or Mohammedans, are in bondage to Satan,—in the bondage of transgression and sin,—and are to be cast out. "Every one that committeth sin is the bond-servant of sin. And the bond-servant abideth not in the house forever; the son abideth forever." Thank God, then, for "the adoption of sons."

"Two Sons"

Those false teachers would persuade the brethren that in turning from whole-hearted faith in Christ and trusting to works which they themselves could do, they would become children of Abraham, and so heirs of the promises. They forgot that Abraham had two sons. I myself have talked with a Jew according to the flesh, who did not know that Abraham had more than one son; and there are many Christians who seem to think that to be descended from Abraham, after the flesh, is all-sufficient to insure one a share {184} in the promised inheritance. "They which are the children of the flesh, these are not the children of God; but the children of the promise are counted for the seed." Rom. 9:8. Now of the two sons of Abraham, one was born after the flesh, and the other was by promise, born of the Spirit. "By faith even Sarah herself received power to conceive seed when she was past age, since she counted Him faithful who had promised." Heb. 11:11, R.V. Hagar was an Egyptian slave. The children of a slave woman are always slaves, even though their father be a freeman; and so Hagar could bring forth children only to bondage. But long before Ishmael was born, the Lord had plainly signified to Abraham, who wished that his servant Eliezer might be his heir, that it was not a bond-servant, even though born in his house, that He had promised him, but a free-born son,—a son born of a freewoman. God has no slaves in His kingdom.

"These Are the Two Covenants"

What are the two covenants?—The two women, Hagar and Sarah; for we read that Hagar is Mount Sinai, "which gendereth to bondage." That is, just as Hagar could not bring forth any other kind of children than slaves, so the law, even the law that God spoke from Sinai, can not beget freemen. It can do nothing but hold them in bondage. "The law worketh wrath:" "for by the law is the knowledge of sin." The same is true of the covenant from Sinai, for it consisted merely of the promise of the people to keep that law, and had, {185} therefore, no more power to make them free than the law itself had,—no more power than they already had in their bondage. Nay, rather, it "gendered to bondage," since their making it was simply a promise to make themselves righteous by their own works, and man in himself is "without strength."

Consider the situation: The people were in the bondage of sin; they had no power to break their chains; but the speaking of the law made no change in their condition; it introduced no new feature. If a man is in prison for crime, you can not release him by reading the statutes to him. It was the law that put him there, and the reading of it to him only makes his captivity more painful.

"Then did not God Himself lead them into bondage?"—Not by any means; since He did not induce them to make that covenant at Sinai. Four hundred and thirty years before that time He had made a covenant with Abraham, which was sufficient for all purposes. That covenant was confirmed in Christ, and, therefore, was a covenant from above. See n 8:23. It promised righteousness as a free gift of God through faith, and it included all nations. All the miracles that God had wrought in delivering the children of Israel from Egyptian bondage were but demonstrations of His power to deliver them and us from the bondage of sin. Yes, the deliverance from Egypt was itself a demonstration not only of God's power, but also of His desire to lead them from the bondage of sin, that bondage in which the covenant from Sinai holds men, because Hagar, who is the covenant from Sinai, was an Egyptian. So when {186} the people came to Sinai, God simply referred them to what He had already done, and then said, "Now therefore, if ye will obey My voice indeed, and keep My covenant, then ye shall be a peculiar treasure unto Me above all people; for all the earth is Mine." Ex. 19:5. To what covenant did He refer?—Evidently to the one already in existence, His covenant with Abraham. If they would simply keep God's covenant, that is, God's promise,—keep the faith,—they would be a peculiar treasure unto God, for God, as the possessor of all the earth, was able to do with them all that He had promised. The fact that they in their self-sufficiency rashly took the whole responsibility upon themselves, does not prove that God led them into making that covenant, but the contrary. He was leading them out of bondage, not into it, and the apostle plainly tells us that covenant from Sinai was nothing but bondage.

Further, if the children of Israel who came out of Egypt had but walked "in the steps of that faith of our father Abraham, which he had being yet uncircumcised" (Rom. 4:12), the law would never have been spoken from Sinai; "for the promise, that he should be the heir of the world, was not to Abraham, or to his seed, through the law, but through the righteousness of faith" (Rom. 4:13). Faith justifies, makes righteous; if the people had had Abraham's faith, they would have had the righteousness that he had; and then there would have been no occasion for the entering of the law, which was "spoken because of transgression." The law would have been in their hearts, and they would not {187} have needed to be awakened by its thunders to a sense of their condition. God never expected, and does not now expect, that any person can get righteousness by the law proclaimed from Sinai; and everything connected with

Sinai shows it. Yet the law is truth, and must be kept. God delivered the people from Egypt, "that they might observe His statutes, and keep His laws." Ps. 105:45. We do not get life by keeping the commandments, but God gives us life in order that we may keep them.

The Two Covenants Parallel

Note the statement which the apostle makes when speaking of the two women, Hagar and Sarah: "These are the two covenants." So then the two covenants existed in every essential particular in the days of Abraham. Even so they do today; for the Scripture says now as well as then, "Cast out the bond-woman and her son." We see then that the two covenants are not matters of time, but of condition. Let no one flatter himself that he can not be under the old covenant, because the time for that is passed. The time for that is passed only in the sense that "the time past of our life may suffice us to have wrought the will of the Gentiles, when we walked in lasciviousness, lusts, excess of wine, revelings, banquetings, and abominable idolatries." 1 Pet. 4:3.

Difference Between the Two

The difference is just the difference between a freewoman and a slave. Hagar's children, no matter how many she might have had, would have been slaves, while those of Sarah would necessarily be free. {188}

So the covenant from Sinai holds all who adhere to it in bondage "under the law;" while the covenant from above gives freedom, not freedom from obedience to the law, but freedom from disobedience to it. The freedom is not found away from the law, but in the law. Christ redeems from the curse, which is the transgression of the law. He redeems us from the curse, that the blessing may come on us; and the blessing is obedience to the law. "Blessed are the undefiled in the way, who walk in the law of the Lord." Ps. 119:1. This blessedness is freedom. "I will walk at liberty; for I seek Thy precepts." Ps. 119:45.

The difference between the two covenants may be put briefly thus: In the covenant from Sinai we ourselves have to do with the law alone, while in the covenant from above, we have the law in Christ. In the first instance it is death to us, since the law is sharper than any two-edged sword, and we are not able to handle it without fatal results; but in the second instance we have the law "in the hand of a Mediator." In the one case it is what we can do; in the other case it is what the Spirit of God can do. Bear in mind that there is not the slightest question in the whole Epistle to the Galatians as to whether or not the law should be kept. The only question is, How shall it be done? Is it to be our own doing, so that the reward shall not be of grace but of debt? or is it to be God working in us both to will and to do of His good pleasure? {189}

Mount Sinai and Mount Zion

"This Agar is Mount Sinai in Arabia, and answereth to Jerusalem which now is, and is in bondage with her children. But Jerusalem which is above is free, which is the mother of us all." As there are the two covenants, so there are two cities to which they pertain. Jerusalem which now is pertains to the old covenant—to Mount Sinai. It will never be free, but will be replaced by the city of God, the heavenly Jerusalem, "which cometh down out of heaven." Rev. 3:12; 21:1–5. It is the city for which Abraham looked, the "city which hath foundations, whose builder and maker is God." Heb. 11:10; Rev. 21:14. There are many who build great hopes—all their hope—on Jerusalem which now is. For such the veil remaineth "untaken away in the reading of the old testament." 2 Cor. 3:14. They are in reality looking to Mount Sinai and the old covenant for salvation, and it is not to be found there. "For ye are not come unto the mount that might be touched, and that burned with fire, nor unto blackness, and darkness, and tempest, and the sound of a trumpet, and the voice of words; which voice they that heard entreated that the word should not be spoken to them any more (for they could not endure that which was commanded, And if so much as a beast touch the mountain, it shall be stoned, or thrust through with a dart; and so terrible was the sight, that Moses said, I exceedingly fear and quake); but ye are come unto Mount Sion, and unto the city of the living God, the heavenly Jerusalem, and to an innumerable company of angels, to the {190} general assembly and church of the first-born, which are written in heaven, and to God the Judge of all, and to the spirits of just men made perfect, and to Jesus the Mediator of the new covenant, and to the blood of sprinkling, that speaketh better things than that of Abel." Heb. 12:18–24.

Whoever looks to the present Jerusalem for blessings, is looking to the old covenant, to Mount Sinai, to bondage; whoever worships with his face toward the New Jerusalem, and who expects blessings only from it, is looking to the new covenant, to Mount Zion, to freedom; for "Jerusalem which is above is free." From what is it free?—Free from sin; and since it is our mother, it begets us anew, so that we also become free from sin. Free from the law?—Yes, certainly, for the law has no condemnation for them who are in Christ Jesus.

But do not let anybody deceive you with vain words, telling you that you may now trample God's law underfoot,—that law which He Himself proclaimed in such awful majesty from Sinai.

Coming to Mount Sion,—to Jesus, the Mediator of the new covenant, and to the blood of sprinkling,—we become free from sin,—from transgression of the law. The basis of God's throne in Zion is His law. From the throne proceed the same "lightnings and thunderings and voices" (Rev. 4:5; 11:19) as from Sinai, because the selfsame law is there. But it is "the throne of grace," and, therefore, in spite of the thunders, we come to it boldly, assured that from God, the Judge of all, who sits upon the mercy-seat, we shall obtain mercy. Nay, more, we shall also find grace {191} to help in time of need,—grace to help us in the hour of temptation to sin,—for out of the midst of the throne, from the slain Lamb (Rev. 5:6), flows the river of water of life, bringing to us from the heart of Christ "the law of the Spirit of life." We drink of it, we bathe in it, and we find cleansing from all sin.

"Why didn't the Lord bring the people directly to Mount Zion then, where they could find the law as life, and not to Mount Sinai, where it was only death?"

That is a very natural question, and one that is easily answered. It was because of their unbelief. When God brought Israel out of Egypt, it was His purpose to bring them to Mount Zion as directly as they could go. When they had crossed the Red Sea, they sang an inspired song, of which this was a part: "Thou in Thy mercy hast led forth the people which Thou hast redeemed; Thou hast guided them in Thy strength unto Thy holy habitation." "Thou shalt bring them in, and plant them in the mountain of Thine inheritance, in the place, O Lord, which Thou hast made for Thee to dwell in, in the sanctuary, O Lord, which Thy hands have established." Ex. 15:13,17. If they had continued singing, they would very soon have come to Zion; for the redeemed of the Lord "come with singing unto Zion," and everlasting joy is upon their heads. Is. 35:10; 51:11. The dividing of the Red Sea was the proof of this. See verse 10. But they soon forgot the Lord, and murmured in unbelief. Therefore "the law was added because of transgressions." It was their own fault— the result of their sinful unbelief— {192} that they came to Mount Sinai instead of to Mount Zion.

Nevertheless, God did not leave Himself without witness of His faithfulness. At Mount Sinai the law was in the hand of the same Mediator, Jesus, to whom we come when we come to Zion; and from the Rock in Horeb, which is Sinai, flowed the living stream, the water of life from the heart of Christ. Ex. 17:6; 1 Cor. 10:4. There they had not merely the picture, but the reality, of Mount Zion. Every soul whose heart there turned to the Lord, would have beheld His unveiled glory, even as Moses did, and, being transformed by it, would have found the ministration of righteousness, instead of the ministration of condemnation.

"His mercy endureth forever;" and even upon the clouds of wrath from which proceed the thunders and lightnings of the law, shines the glorious face of the Sun of Righteousness, and forms the bow of promise.

"The Son Abideth Ever"

"Cast out the bondwoman and her son; for the son of the bondwoman shall not be heir with the son of the freewoman." "The bond-servant abideth not in the house forever; the son abideth forever." n 8:35, R.V. Here is comfort for every soul. You are a sinner, or, at best, "trying to be a Christian," and you tremble with terror at these words, as you realize that you are in bondage,—that sin has a hold upon you, and you are bound by the cords of evil habits. Ah, you must learn not to be afraid when the Lord speaks, for He speaks peace, even though it be with a voice of thunder! The more majestic the {193} voice, the greater the peace that He gives. Take courage! The son of the bondwoman is the flesh and its works. "Flesh and blood can not inherit the kingdom of God; neither doth corruption inherit incorruption." But God says, "Cast out the bondwoman and her son," and if you are willing that His will shall be done in you as it is done in heaven, He will see that the flesh and its works are cast out from you, and you will be "delivered from the bondage of corruption into the glorious liberty of the children of God." That command which so frightened you is simply the voice commanding the evil spirit to depart, and to come no more into you. It speaks to you victory over every sin. Receive Christ by faith, and you have the power to become the son of God, heir of a kingdom which can not be moved, but which, with all its people, abideth forever.

"Stand Fast, Therefore"

Where shall we stand?—"In the liberty wherewith Christ hath made us free." And what freedom is that?—It is the freedom of Christ Himself, whose delight was in the law of the Lord, because it was in His heart. Ps. 40:8. "The law of the Spirit of life in Christ Jesus hath made me free from the law of sin and death." Rom. 8:2.

We stand only by faith.

In this freedom there is no trace of bondage. It is perfect liberty. It is liberty of soul, liberty of thought, as well as liberty of action. It is not that we are simply given the ability to keep the law, but we are given the mind that finds delight in doing it. It is not that we comply with the law because we see {194} no other way of escape from punishment; that would be galling bondage. It is from such bondage that God's covenant releases us. No; the promise of God, when accepted, puts the mind of the Spirit into us, so that we find the highest pleasure in obedience to all the precepts of God's Word. The soul is as free as a bird soaring above the mountain-tops. It is the glorious liberty of the children of God, who have the full range of "the breadth, and length, and depth, and height" of God's universe. It is the liberty of those who do not have to be watched, but who can be trusted anywhere, since their every step is but the movement of God's own holy law. Why be content with bondage, when such limitless freedom is yours? The prison doors are open; walk out into God's freedom.

"Out of my shameful failure and loss,
Jesus, I come. Jesus, I come.
Into the glorious gain of Thy cross,
Jesus, I come to Thee.
Out of earth's sorrows, into Thy balm,
Out of life's storm, and into Thy calm,
Out of distress to jubilant psalm,
Jesus, I come to Thee.
"Out of unrest and arrogant pride,
Jesus, I come. Jesus, I come.
Into Thy blessed will to abide,
Jesus, I come to Thee.
Out of myself to dwell in Thy love,
Out of despair into raptures above,
Upward for aye on wings like a dove,
Jesus, I come to Thee." {195}

The Spirit's Power Over The Flesh

WITH freedom did Christ set us free; stand fast therefore, and be not entangled again in a yoke of bondage.

"Behold, I Paul say unto you, that, if ye receive circumcision, Christ will profit you nothing. Yea, I testify again to every man that receiveth circumcision, that he is a debtor to do the whole law. Ye are severed from Christ, ye who would be justified by the law; ye are fallen away from grace. For we through the Spirit by faith wait for the hope of righteousness. For in Christ Jesus neither circumcision availeth anything, nor uncircumcision; but faith working through love. Ye were running well; who did hinder you that ye should not obey the truth? This persuasion came not of him that calleth you. A little leaven leaveneth the whole lump. I have confidence to you-ward in the Lord, that ye will be none otherwise minded; but he that troubleth you shall bear his judgment, whosoever he be. But I, brethren, if I still preach circumcision, why am I still persecuted? then hath the stumbling-block of the cross been done away. I would that they which unsettle you would even cut themselves off.

"For ye, brethren, were called for freedom; only use not your freedom for an occasion to the flesh, but through love be servants one to another. For the {196} whole law is fulfilled in one word, even in this: Thou shalt love thy neighbor as thyself. But if ye bite and devour one another, take heed that ye be not consumed one of another.

"But I say, Walk by the Spirit, and ye shall not fulfill the lust of the flesh. For the flesh lusteth against the Spirit, and the Spirit against the flesh; for these are contrary the one to the other; that ye may not do the things that ye would. But if ye are led by the Spirit, ye are not under the law. Now the works of the flesh are manifest, which are these, fornication, uncleanness, lasciviousness, idolatry, sorcery, enmities, strife, jealousies, wraths, factions, divisions, heresies, envyings, drunkenness, revelings, and such like; of the which I forewarn you, even as I did forewarn you, that they which practice such things shall not inherit the kingdom of God. But the fruit of the Spirit is love, joy, peace, long-suffering, kindness, goodness, faithfulness, meekness, temperance; against such there is no law. And they that are of Christ Jesus have crucified the flesh with the passions and the lusts thereof.

"If we live by the Spirit, by the Spirit let us also walk. Let us not be vainglorious, provoking one another, envying one another." Galatians 5, R.V.

The connection between the fourth and fifth chapters of Galatians is closer than between any other two, so much so that it is difficult to see how anybody could ever have hit upon the idea of making a chapter division. One can not possibly close his reading of the fourth chapter with the thirty-first {197} verse, but must take in the first verse of the fifth chapter, as we have done. But we have not by any means learned all from that verse that we may, and we therefore dwell upon it longer.

The Freedom That Christ Gives

When Christ was manifest in the flesh, His work was to proclaim "deliverance to the captives," and "to set at liberty them that are bruised." The miracles that He performed were practical illustrations of this work, and one of the most striking may well be considered at this stage of our study.

"And He was teaching in one of the synagogues on the Sabbath. And, behold, there was a woman which had a spirit of infirmity eighteen years, and was bowed together, and could in nowise lift up herself. And when Jesus saw her, He called her to Him, and said unto her, Woman, thou art loosed from thine infirmity. And He laid His hands on her; and immediately she was made straight, and glorified God." Luke 13:10–13.

Then when the hypocritical ruler of the synagogue complained because Jesus did this miracle on the Sabbath, He referred to how each one would loose his ox or ass from the stall, and lead him to water, and then said:—

"And ought not this woman, being a daughter of Abraham, whom Satan hath bound, lo, these eighteen years, be loosed from this bond on the Sabbath day?"

Two features in this case are worthy of special note: The woman was bound by Satan, and she had a spirit of infirmity, or absence of strength. {198}

Now note how accurately this describes our condition before we meet Christ.

1. We are bound by Satan, "taken captive by him at his will." "Every one that committeth sin is the bond-servant of sin" (n 8:34), and "he that committeth sin is of the devil" (1 . 3:8). "His own iniquities shall take the wicked himself, and he shall be holden with the cords of his sins." Prov. 5:22. Sin is the cord with which Satan binds us.

2. We have a spirit of infirmity, and can in nowise lift ourselves up, or free ourselves from the chains that bind us. It was when we were "without strength" that Christ died for us.

Rom. 5:6. Now these two words, "without strength," are translated from the very same word that is rendered "infirmity" in the account of the woman whom Jesus healed. She was "without strength." To be without strength means to have no strength at all. That is our condition.

What Jesus Does for Us

What now does Jesus do for us?—He takes the weakness, and gives us in return His strength. "We have not an High Priest which can not be touched with the feeling of our infirmities." Heb. 4:15. "Himself took our infirmities, and bare our sicknesses." Matt. 8:17. He becomes all that we are, in order that we may become all that He is. He was "born under the law, to redeem them that were under the law." He hath delivered us from the curse, being made a curse for us, that the blessing might come to us. Although He knew no sin, He {199} was made to be sin for us, "that we might be made the righteousness of God in Him." 2 Cor. 5:21.

Why He Does It

Why did Jesus make that woman free from her infirmity?—In order that she might walk at liberty. Certainly it was not in order that she might continue of her own free will to do that which before she was obliged to do. And why does He make us free from sin?—In order that we may live free from sin. On account of the weakness of our flesh, we are unable to do the righteousness of the law; therefore Christ, who is come in the flesh, and who has power over all flesh, strengthens us with might by His Spirit in the inner man, that the righteousness of the law may be fulfilled in us, who walk not after the flesh, but after the Spirit. We can not tell how He does it; He alone knows how it is done, because He alone has the power; but we may know the reality of it.

Present Freedom

Pay special attention to the words of Jesus to the woman, uttered while she was yet bound down, and unable to lift herself up: "Thou art loosed from thine infirmity." "Thou art loosed," present tense. That is just what He says to us. To every captive He has proclaimed deliverance. The woman "could in nowise lift up herself;" yet at the word of Christ she at once stood erect. She could not do it, yet she did. The things that are impossible for men are possible for God. "The Lord upholdeth all that fall, and raiseth up all those that be bowed down." Ps. 145:14. Faith does not make facts; it only lays hold {200} of them. There is not a single soul that is bowed down with the weight of sin which Satan hath bound on him, whom Christ does not lift up. Freedom is his; he has only to make use of it. Let the message be sounded far and wide. Let every soul hear it, that Christ has given deliverance to every captive. Thousands will rejoice at the news.

Christ came to restore that which was lost; He redeems us from the curse; He hath redeemed us; therefore the liberty wherewith He makes us free is the liberty that existed before the curse came. Man was made a king. It was not merely the one individual first created who was made king, but all mankind. "In the day that God created man, in the likeness of God made He him; male and female created He them; and blessed them, and called their name Adam," that is, man. Gen. 5:1,2. "And God said, Let us make man in our image, after our likeness; and let them have dominion over the fish of the sea, and over the fowl of the air, and over the cattle, and over all the earth, and over every creeping thing that creepeth upon the earth. So God created man in His own image, in the image of God created He him; male and female created He them. And God blessed them, and God said unto them, Be fruitful, and multiply, and replenish the earth, and subdue it; and have dominion," etc. The dominion, we see, was given to every human being, male and female.

This dominion was universal. When God made man, He "put all things in subjection under his feet. For in that He put all in subjection under him, He {201} left nothing that is not put under him." Heb. 2:8. The dominion was not confined to this planet; for when God crowned man with glory and honor, He set him over the works of His hands (Heb. 2:7), and we read, "Thou, Lord, in the beginning hast laid the foundation of the earth; and the heavens are the works of Thine hands" (Heb. 1:10). This shows how free man was before the curse came; for it is self-evident that a ruler must have absolute freedom, at least as far as his dominion extends, else he is not ruler.

It is true that now we do not see all things put under man; "but we behold Him who hath been made a little lower than the angels, even Jesus, because of the suffering of death crowned with glory and honor, that by the grace of God He should taste death for every man" (Heb. 2:9, R.V.), and thus redeem every man from the curse of the lost dominion. "Crowned with glory and honor." A crown implies kingship, and Christ's crown is that which man had when he was set over the works of God's hands. Accordingly, Christ (as man, mind you, in the flesh), just as He was about to ascend to heaven after the resurrection, said: "All power is given unto Me in heaven and in earth. Go ye therefore." Matt. 28:18,19. This indicates that the same power is given to us in Him; and this is made certain by the inspired prayer that we might know the exceeding greatness of God's power in us who believe, "according to the working of His mighty power, which He wrought in Christ, when He raised Him from the dead, and set Him at His own right hand in the heavenly places, far above {202} all principality, and power, and might, and dominion, and every name that is named, not only in this world, but also in that which is to come; and hath put all things under His feet;" and this prayer is followed by the statement that God has made us alive in Christ, and "raised us up together, and made us sit together in heavenly places in Christ Jesus." Eph. 1:18–22; 2:1–6.

Christ has tasted death for us as man, and through the cross has redeemed us from the curse. If we are crucified with Him, we are also risen with Him, and made to sit together with Him in the heavenly places, with all things under our feet. If we do not know this, it is only because we have not allowed the Spirit to reveal it to us. The eyes of our heart need to be enlightened by the Spirit, that we may know what is "the hope of His calling, and what the riches of the glory of His inheritance in the saints." The exhortation to those who are dead and risen with Christ is, "Let not sin therefore reign in your mortal body, that ye should obey it in the lusts thereof." Rom. 6:12. That shows that we are masters. We have authority over sin, that it shall have no dominion over us.

We have redemption through the blood of Christ, even the forgiveness of sin (Eph. 1:7); and when He "washed us from our sins in His own blood," He "made us kings and priests unto God and His Father." Rev. 1:5,6. Glorious dominion! Glorious freedom! Freedom from the power of the curse, even while surrounded by it; freedom from "this present evil world,"—the lust of the flesh, the lust of the {203} eyes, and the pride of life! The freedom of the universe (power in heaven and on earth), so that neither "the prince of the power of the air" nor the "rulers of the darkness of this world" can have any dominion over us! It is the freedom and authority that Christ had when He said, "Get thee hence, Satan." And the devil immediately left Him. It is authority "over all the power of the enemy." Luke 10:19. It is such freedom that nothing in heaven or earth can coerce us, to make us do anything against our will. God will not attempt it, for we hold our freedom from Him; and no one else can do it. It is power over the elements, so that they will serve us, instead of controlling us. We shall learn to recognize Christ and His cross in everything, so that the curse will be powerless over us, and our minds and bodies will not be subject to every change in the weather. Our health will spring forth speedily; for the life of Jesus will be manifest in our mortal flesh. Such glorious liberty no tongue or pen can describe. Believe in it as the Holy Spirit makes it known, accept it, and stand fast in it; yea, stand fast!

"By the word of the Lord were the heavens made; and all the host of them by the breath of His mouth." "He spake, and it was done; He commanded, and it stood fast." Ps. 33:6,9. The same word that created the starry host, speaks to us, "Stand fast!" It is not a command that leaves us as helpless as before, but one which carries the performance of the act with it. Recall the cases of the lame men who were {204} healed. John 5:5–9; Acts 3:2–8; 14:8–10. The command does the thing commanded. The heavens did not create themselves, but were brought into existence by the word of the Lord. Then let them be your teachers. "Lift up your eyes on high, and see who hath created these, that bringeth out their host by number; He calleth them all by name; by the greatness of His might, and for that He is strong in power, not one is lacking." Is. 40:26, R.V. "He giveth power to the faint; and to them that have no might He increaseth strength." Is. 40:29. Listen to the words, "Stand fast!"

A Question of Profit

"If ye receive circumcision, Christ will profit you nothing." It should be understood that much more is involved than the mere rite of circumcision. The proof of this is found in the fact that this Epistle, which has so much to say about circumcision, has been preserved by the Lord for us, and contains the Gospel message for all time; yet circumcision as a rite is not a burning, living question now. Nobody is seeking to have Christians submit to the rite of circumcision in the flesh.

The question under consideration is how to obtain righteousness—salvation from sin—and the inheritance of righteousness. The fact is that it can be obtained only by faith—by receiving Christ into the heart, and allowing Him to live His life in us. Abraham had this righteousness of God by faith of Jesus Christ, and God gave Him circumcision as a sign of that fact. It had a peculiar significance to {205} Abraham, serving continually to remind him of his failure, when he tried, by means of the flesh, to fulfil God's promise. The record of it serves the same purpose for us. It signifies that "the flesh profiteth nothing," and is not, therefore, to be depended on. The mere fact of being circumcised did not make Christ of no avail, for Paul was himself circumcised, and as a matter of expediency he had Timothy circumcised. Acts 16:1–3. But Paul did not count his circumcision nor any other external thing of any value (Phil. 3:4–7), and when it was proposed to circumcise Titus, as a thing necessary to salvation, he would not allow it (Gal. 2:3–5).

That which was to be only the sign of an already-existing fact, was taken by subsequent generations as the means of establishing the fact. Circumcision, therefore, stands in this Epistle as the representative of all kinds of work done by men with a view of obtaining righteousness. Outward circumcision, in the flesh, which was what Judaizing teachers were seeking to impose on believers from among the Gentiles as the great means of salvation (see Acts 15:1), stands for the works of the flesh, as opposed to the Spirit.

Now the truth is stated that if a person does anything with the expectation of being saved by it, that is, of getting salvation by his own work, Christ profits him nothing. If Christ be not accepted as a complete Redeemer, He is not accepted at all. That is to say, if Christ be not accepted for what He is, He is rejected. He can not be other than what He is. Christ is not divided; and He does not share {206} with any other person or thing the honor of being Saviour. Therefore it is easy to see that if any one were circumcised with a view to receiving salvation thereby, that would show absence of faith in Christ as the all-sufficient and only Saviour of mankind.

God gave circumcision as a sign of faith in Christ; the Jews perverted it into a substitute for faith. So when a Jew boasted in his circumcision, he was boasting of his own righteousness. This is shown by verse 4: "Christ is become of no effect unto you, whosoever of you are justified by the law; ye are fallen from grace." This is no disparagement of the law, but of man's ability to keep the law. It is the glory of the law that it is so holy, and its requirements are so great, that no man is able to attain to the perfection of it. Only in Christ is the righteousness of the law ours; and true circumcision is to worship God in Spirit, to rejoice in Christ Jesus, and to put no confidence in the flesh. Phil. 3:3.

In Debt to the Law

"I testify again to every man that is circumcised, that he is a debtor to do the whole law."

"There!" exclaims some one, "that shows that the law is a thing to be avoided; for Paul says that those who are circumcised have got to do the whole law; and he warns them not to be circumcised."

Not quite so hasty, my friend. Stick a little more closely to the text. Read it again, and you will see that the bad thing is not the law, nor the doing of the law, but that the thing to be avoided is being a debtor to the law. Is there not a vast difference? It is a {207} good thing to have food to eat and clothes to wear, but it is a sorrowful thing to be in debt for these necessary things. Sadder yet is it to be in debt for them, and yet to lack them.

A debtor is one who owes something. He who is in debt to the law, owes what the law demands, namely, righteousness. Therefore, whoever is in debt to the law is under the curse; for it is written, "Cursed is every one that continueth not in all things that are written in the book of the law to do them." So to attempt to get righteousness by any other means than by faith in Christ is to incur the curse of eternal debt. He is eternally in debt, for he has nothing wherewith to pay; yet the fact that he is in debt to the law,—debtor to do the whole law,—shows that he ought to do it all. How shall he do it?—"This is the work of God, that ye believe on Him whom He hath sent." n 6:29. Let him cease trusting in himself, and receive and confess Christ in his flesh, and then the righteousness of the law will be fulfilled in him, because he will not walk after the flesh, but after the Spirit.

"The Hope of Righteousness by Faith"

"For we through the Spirit wait for the hope of righteousness by faith." Don't pass this verse by without reading it more than once, or you will think that it says something that it does not say. And as you read it, think of what you have already learned about the promise of the Spirit.

Don't imagine that this verse teaches that, having the Spirit, we must wait for righteousness. Not by {208} any means; the Spirit brings righteousness. "The Spirit is life because of righteousness." Rom. 8:10. When He is come, He will convince the world of sin and of righteousness. n 16:8. Whoever, therefore, receives the Spirit, has the conviction of sin, and has also the righteousness which the Spirit shows him that he lacks, and which the Spirit alone can bring.

What is the righteousness which the Spirit brings?—It is the righteousness of the law; this we know, "for we know that the law is spiritual." Rom. 7:14.

What, then, about the "hope of righteousness," for which we wait through the Spirit? Notice that it does not say that we through the Spirit hope for righteousness, but that we wait for the hope of righteousness by faith, that is, the hope which the possession of righteousness brings. Let us briefly go over this matter in detail. It will not take long, for we have already studied it, and all that we have to do is to refresh our minds.

1. The Spirit of God is "the Holy Spirit of promise." Not the Spirit promised, but the Spirit the possession of whom insures to us the promise of God.

2. That which God has promised to us, as children of Abraham, is an inheritance. The Holy Spirit is the earnest or pledge of this inheritance, until the purchased possession is redeemed and bestowed upon us. Eph. 1:13,14.

3. This inheritance that is promised is the new heavens and the new earth, "wherein dwelleth righteousness." 2 Pet. 3:13.

4. The Spirit brings righteousness; for the Spirit {209} is Christ's representative, the means by which Christ Himself,

who is our righteousness, comes to dwell in our hearts. n 14:16–18.

5. Therefore the hope which the Spirit brings is the hope which the possession of righteousness brings, namely, the hope of an inheritance in the kingdom of God, the earth made new.

6. The righteousness which the Spirit brings to us is the righteousness of the law of God, which by the Spirit is written in our hearts, instead of on tables of stone. Rom. 2:29; 2 Cor. 3:3.

7. The sum of the whole matter, therefore, is this, that if we will wholly distrust ourselves, and will acknowledge that in us there dwelleth no good thing, and that consequently no good thing can come from us; and so, instead of thinking ourselves so powerful that we can do the law, will allow the Holy Spirit to fill us, that thus we may be filled with the righteousness of the law, we shall have living hope dwelling in us. The hope of the Spirit—the hope of righteousness by faith—has no element of uncertainty in it; it is positive assurance. But in nothing else is there any hope. He who has not "the righteousness which is of God by faith," has no hope whatever. Only Christ in us is "the hope of glory."

No Power Except in Faith

"For in Jesus Christ neither circumcision availeth anything, nor uncircumcision; but faith which worketh by love." The word here rendered "availeth" is the same word that is rendered "able" in Luke 13:24; Acts 15:10; 6:10. In Phil. 4:13 it is {210} rendered "can do." The statement, therefore, amounts to this: Circumcision is not able to do anything, neither is uncircumcision; but faith alone, which works by love, can do anything. This faith which works by love is found only in Christ Jesus.

But what is it that there is talk about doing?—Nothing else than the law of God. No man can do it, whatever his state or condition. The uncircumcised man has no power to keep the law, and circumcision has no power to enable him to do it. One may boast of his circumcision, and another may boast of his uncircumcision, but both are alike vain. By the law of faith boasting is excluded (Rom. 3:27); for since the faith of Christ alone can keep the righteousness of the law, there is no chance for us to tell what we have done.

"All to Christ I owe"

Hindered

The Galatian brethren had started well, for they had "begun in the Spirit;" but somebody had hindered them in the way. The question is, "Who did hinder you that ye should not obey the truth?" God's law is the truth (Ps. 119:142), and the Galatian brethren had started out to obey it; they had succeeded in the beginning, but later on had been hindered in their progress. Why?—"Because they sought it not by faith, but as it were by the works of the law. For they stumbled at that stumbling-stone." Christ is the way, and the truth, and the life, and there is no stumbling in Him. He is made unto us righteousness; the perfection of the law is in Him, for His life is the law. {211}

"The Offense of the Cross"

The cross is and always has been a symbol of disgrace. To be crucified was to be subjected to the most ignominious death known. The apostle said that if he preached circumcision, that is, righteousness by works, the offense of the cross would cease. The offense of the cross is that it is a confession of human frailty and sin, and of inability to do any good thing. To take the cross of Christ means to depend solely on Him for everything, and this is the abasement of all human pride. Men love to fancy themselves independent. They have no objection to any good-ness that they themselves can do. One might preach "morality" to a band of robbers, or to any heathen, and it would be well received, so long as they were exhorted to get it by their own efforts. Indeed, they would feel flattered, rather than otherwise, for such preaching would imply that they were already right-eous in themselves. But let the cross be preached; let it be made known that in man dwelleth no good thing, and that all must be received as a gift, and straightway somebody is offended.

Liberty to Serve, Not to Sin

"For, brethren, ye have been called unto liberty; only use not liberty for an occasion to the flesh; but by love serve one another." The two preceding chapters tell about bondage, im-prisonment. Before faith comes, we are shut up under sin, debtors to the law. The faith of Christ sets us free, but as we are set at liberty, the admonition is given us, "Go, and sin no more." We have been set at {212} liberty from sin, not at liberty to sin. How many make a mistake here! Many sincere people imagine that in Christ we are at liberty to ignore the law, and to set it at defiance, forgetting that the transgression of the law is sin. 1 . 3:4. To serve the flesh is to commit sin, "because the carnal mind is enmity against God; for it is not subject to the law of God, neither indeed can be." Rom. 8:7. So when the apostle exhorts us not to use our liberty for an occasion of the flesh, he simply warns us not to misuse the liberty which Christ gives us, and to bring ourselves into bondage again by transgressing the law. Instead of this, we should by love serve one another; for love is the fulfilling of the law.

Recall what has been said in this chapter concerning the liberty wherewith Christ makes us free. He gives us the liberty of the first dominion. But remember that God gave the dominion to mankind, and that in Christ all are made kings. This shows that the only human being over whom any Christian has the right to rule is himself. The great man in Christ's kingdom is he who rules his own spirit. As kings, our subjects are found in the lower orders of created beings, in the elements, and in our own flesh, but not in our fellow-men. We are to serve them. We are to have in us the mind that was in Christ while He was still in the royal court in heaven, "in the form of God," which led Him to take "the form of a servant." Phil. 2:5–7. He did not change His nature in coming to this earth, but only His form; therefore, as Anointed King in Zion, He was a servant. This is further seen by the fact that {213} He washed the feet of the disciples, with full consciousness of the fact that He was their Master and Lord, and that He came from God and went to God. John 13:3–13. Moreover, when all the redeemed saints appear in glory, Christ Himself "shall gird Himself, and make them to sit down to meat, and will come forth and serve them." Luke 12:37. The greatest freedom is found in service—in service rendered to our fellows in the name of Jesus. He who does the greatest service—not greatest as men reckon, but what they would call lowest—is the greatest. This we learn from Christ, who is King of kings and Lord of lords, because He is servant of all, performing service that nobody else would or could do. God's servants are all kings.

Love Fulfills the Law

Love is not a substitute for the keeping of the law, but is the perfection of it. Just here it would be well to read 1 Cor. 13. "Love worketh no ill to his neighbor; therefore love is the fulfilling of the law." Rom. 13:10. "If any man say, I love God, and hateth his brother, he is a liar; for he that loveth not his brother whom he hath seen, how can he love God whom he hath not seen?" 1 . 4:20. If, therefore, a man loves his neighbor it must be that he loves God. "Love is of God," for "God is love." Therefore love is the life of God. If that life be in us, and be given free course, the law will necessarily be in us, for God's life is the law for all creation. That life of love was manifested in the gift of Himself for the world. "Hereby perceive we the love of {214} God, because He laid down His life for us; and we ought to lay down our lives for the brethren."

Love Is Unselfishness

This follows from the foregoing; for since love means service, and service means the doing of something for others, it is evident that love takes no thought of itself, and that he who loves has no thought but of how he may bless others. So we read, "Love suffereth long, and is kind; love envieth not; love vaunteth not itself, is not puffed up, doth not behave itself unseemly, seeketh not its own, is not provoked, taketh not account of evil." 1 Cor. 13:4,5, R.V.

It is just on this vital point that everybody in the world is making or has made a mistake. Happy are they who have found out their mistake, and have come to the understanding and practice of true love. "Love seeketh not her own." Therefore self-love is not love at all, in the right sense of the word. It is only a base counterfeit. Yet the most of that which in the world is called love, is not really love for another, but is love of self. Even that which should be the highest form of love known on earth, the love which is used by the Lord as a representation of His love for His people,—the love of husband and wife,—is more often selfishness than real love. Leaving out of the question, as unworthy of notice, marriages that are formed for the purpose of gaining wealth or position in society, it is a fact, which all will recognize when their attention is called to it, that in nearly every case the parties to a marriage are thinking more of their own individual happiness than of the {215} happiness of the other. Of course this condition of things exists in varying degrees, and in proportion as real, unselfish love exists, is there real happiness; for it is a lesson that the world is slow to learn, that true happiness is found only when one ceases to seek for it, and sets about making it for others.

"Love Never Faileth"

Here again is a test which shows that much that is called love is not love. Love never ceases. The statement is absolute, never. There is no exception, and no allowance made for circumstances. Love is not affected by circumstances. We often hear about one's love growing cold, but that is something that can never happen. Love is always warm, always flowing; nothing can freeze the fountain of love. Love is absolutely endless and unchangeable, simply because it is the life of God. There is no other love than the love of God, therefore the only possibility for true love to be manifested among mankind is for the love of God to be shed abroad in the heart by the Holy Spirit.

Why Love?

Sometimes when a declaration of love is made, the loved one asks, "Why do you love me?" Just as if anybody could give a reason for love! Love is its own reason. If the lover can tell just why he loves another, then that very answer shows that he does not really love. Whatever object he names as a reason for love, may sometime cease to exist, and then his supposed love ceases to exist; but "love never faileth." Therefore love can not depend upon circumstances. So the {216} only answer that can be given to the question as to why one loves, is "because," because of love. Love loves, simply because it is love. Love is the quality of the individual who loves, and he loves because he has love, irrespective of the character of the object. The truth of this is seen when we go back to God, the Fountain of love. He is love; love is His life; but no explanation of His existence can be given. The highest human conception of love is to love because we are loved, or because the object of our love is lovable. But God loves the unlovely, and those who hate Him. "We also were aforetime foolish, disobedient, deceived, serving divers lusts and pleasures, living in malice and envy, hateful, hating one another. But when the kindness of God our Saviour, and His love toward man, appeared, not by works done in righteousness, which we did ourselves, but according to His mercy He saved us." Titus 3:3,4, R.V. "If ye love them which love you, what reward have ye? do not even the publicans the same?" "Be ye therefore perfect, even as your Father which is in heaven is perfect." Matt. 5:46,48.

Working no Ill

"Love worketh no ill to his neighbor." The word "neighbor" means whoever dwells near. Love, therefore, extends to everything with which it comes in contact. He who loves must necessarily love everybody. It may be objected that love does make distinctions, and the case of husband and wife, or of any of the members of a family, may be cited. But the objection does not hold, for the family relation, rightly understood, was instituted in order that by a union {217} love might the more effectually be manifested to others. On the principle that strength is not merely doubled, but increased tenfold, by union, as shown by the statement that "one shall chase a thousand, and two put ten thousand to flight," union multiplies the working value of love. If two persons, each of whom has this unselfish love to all mankind, unite in love, then their union makes them ten times better able to serve others. If any one thinks this is too high a standard, let him remember that we are considering a very high thing—the highest thing in the universe. We are talking of love, absolute and unqualified, as it comes from heaven, and not that which has been dragged through the mire of earth. Poor, frail human beings certainly need the very best.

Since love worketh no ill to his neighbor, it obviously follows that Christian love,—and there is really no other love, as we have seen,—does not admit of wars and fightings. No philosophy can ever make it appear that it does a man any good to kill him. When the soldiers asked n the Baptist what they should do, as followers of the Lamb of God, to whom he pointed, he replied, "Do violence to no man." Luke 3:14. Those who asked were "soldiers on service," as we see from the margin of the Revised Version. And the margin also gives as the alternative rendering of n's answer, "Put no man in fear." It would be a very mild war in which this command was followed. If an army were composed of Christians,—true followers of Christ,—when they came in contact with the enemy, instead of shooting them, they would find out what {218} they needed, and supply their wants. "If thine enemy hunger, feed him; if he thirst, give him drink; for in so doing thou shalt heap coals of fire on his head. Be not overcome of evil, but overcome evil with good." Rom. 12:20,21.

"Take Heed"

"But if ye bite and devour one another, take heed that ye be not consumed one of another." See into what danger the Galatians had run by following evil counsel. By departing from the simplicity of the faith, they were bringing themselves under the curse, and in danger of hell fire. For "the tongue is a fire, a world of iniquity; so is the tongue among our members, that it defileth the whole body, and setteth on fire the course of nature; and it is set on fire of hell." Jam. 3:6. The tongue has devoured more than the sword, for the sword would never be drawn if it were not for the unruly tongue. No man can tame it, but God can. He had done it in the case of the Galatians, when their mouths were filled with blessing and praise; but what a change had again taken place! As the result of their later instruction, they had descended from blessing to bickering, and instead of talking to edification, were about to devour one another.

"The Leaven of Malice and Wickedness"

Verses 8 and 9, following the question, "Who did hinder you that ye should not obey the truth?" manifestly apply here as well as there, since biting and devouring are very strong evidences of not obeying the truth. "This persuasion cometh not of Him that calleth you." God is the {219} God of peace. Of Christ, the Prince of peace, it was said, "He shall not strive" (Matt. 12:19); therefore "the servant of the Lord must not strive" (2 Tim. 2:24). The Gospel of Jesus Christ is "the Gospel of peace." Eph. 6:15. When there is bickering and strife in the church, be sure that the Gospel has been sadly perverted. Let no one flatter himself on his orthodoxy, or his soundness in the faith, while he has a quarrelsome disposition, or can be provoked to quarrel. Dissension and strife are the marks of departure from the faith, if one was ever in it; for, "being justified by faith, we have peace with God through our Lord Jesus Christ." Rom. 5:1. We are not merely at peace with God, but we have peace with Him—His peace. So this new persuasion, which led to strife and the devouring of one another with the tongue of unholy fire, did not come from God, who had called them into the Gospel. Only a step aside often leads to a wide divergence. Two lines of railway may seem to lie parallel, yet insensibly they diverge until they lead in opposite directions. "A little leaven leaveneth the whole lump." A seemingly "little error," no matter what it be, has in it the germ of all wickedness. "Whosoever shall keep the whole law, and yet offend in one point, he is guilty of all." Jam. 2:10. A single false principle adhered to, will wreck the whole life and character. The little foxes spoil the vines.

The Works of the Flesh

What are the works of the flesh?—Here is a sample list of them: "Adultery, fornication, uncleanness, lasciviousness, idolatry, witchcraft, hatred, {220} variance, emulations, wrath, strife, seditions, heresies, envyings, murders, drunkenness, revelings." Not a pleasant-sounding list, is it? But it is not all of them, for the apostle adds, "and such like." There is a good deal to think about in this list, taken in connection with the statement that "they which do such things shall not inherit the kingdom of God." Compare this list with that given by the Lord in Mark 7:21–23, as the things that come from within, from the heart of man. They are the very life of the natural man. They belong to man by nature. Compare both these lists with the list given in Rom. 1:28–32, as the things done by the heathen, who did not like to retain God in their knowledge. They are the things that are done by all who do not know the Lord.

Then compare these lists of sins with the list given by the apostle Paul in 2 Tim. 3:1–5, of things that will be done in the last days by those who even have a form of godliness. It will be noticed that all these lists are essentially the same. When men turn from "the truth of the Gospel," which is the power of God unto salvation to every one that believeth, they inevitably fall under the power of these sins.

"There Is No Difference."

There is only one flesh of man (1 Cor. 15:39), since all the inhabitants of the earth are descendants of the one pair—Adam and Eve. "By one man sin entered into the world" (Rom. 5:12), so that whatever sin there is in the world is common to all flesh. Therefore it is that in the plan of salvation "there is no difference between the Jew and the {221} Greek; for the same Lord over all is rich unto all that call upon Him." Rom. 10:12. See also Rom. 3:21–24. No person on earth can boast over another, or has any right to despise another because of his sinful, degraded condition. The sight or knowledge of low vices in any people, instead of making us feel complacent over our superior morality, ought, on the contrary, to fill us with sorrow and shame; for it is but a reminder to us of what our human nature is. The works that manifest themselves in that murderer, that drunkard, or that libertine, are simply the works of our flesh. The flesh of mankind has nothing else in its power but just such works as are described in this chapter.

"And Such Like"

Read again that list of the works of the flesh. Some of them are generally recognized as very bad, or, at any rate, as not respectable; but others are commonly regarded as venial sins, if not absolute virtues. Notice, however, the words "and such like," which indicate that all the things here named are identical in character. The Scripture tells us that hatred is murder. "Whosoever hateth his brother is a murderer." 1 . 3:15. Moreover, anger is also murder, as shown by the Saviour in Matt. 5:21,22. Envy, which is so common, also contains murder in it. But who regards emulation as sinful? Isn't emulation encouraged everywhere? Are not children from their infancy taught to strive to surpass somebody else? Is not emulation fostered, not only in schools of all kinds, but also in the home and in the church? In the Sabbath-school, emulation is {222} fostered by the records that are often read out. So far from being regarded as sinful in the extreme, it is cultivated. And yet the Word of God assures us that it is of the same kind as adultery, fornication, murder, and drunkenness, and that they which do such things shall not inherit the kingdom of God. Is it not a fearful thing?

The love of self, the desire for the supremacy, is the source of all the other sins that are mentioned. Out of that have grown innumerable murders; and yet many mothers are unconsciously training their children in that very evil, even while striving to bring them up properly, by saying: "Now see if you can behave better than so and so." "See if you can not learn to read or play better than such an one." "See if you can not keep your clothes looking as nice as that one." All such expressions, which are everyday words in thousands of households, are teaching emulation, setting a false standard. The child is not taught to distinguish between the right and the wrong, and to love the right, but is simply trained to appear better than somebody else. That leads to self-deception and Pharisaism, for all that is thought necessary is to present a better appearance than others, while the heart is corrupt. Those others may not be of very high character, and so the emulator is satisfied, even in this faulty exertion, with simply appearing better than some one who is himself very bad. Go through the entire list, and study each word carefully. Ah, the abominable works of the flesh are lurking where many least suspect them! They are wherever human flesh is, and are manifest {223} in some form or other wherever the flesh is not crucified. Sin coucheth at the door.

The Flesh and the Spirit in Conflict

The flesh and the Spirit of God have nothing in common. They are "contrary the one to the other," that is, they lie over against each other, like two active foes, each eagerly watching the opportunity to crush the other. The flesh is corruption; it can not inherit the kingdom of God, because corruption doth not inherit incorruption. 1 Cor. 15:50. The flesh can not be converted; it must be destroyed. The carnal (fleshly) mind "is enmity against God; for it is not subject to the law of God, neither indeed can be. So then they that are in the flesh can not please God." Rom. 8:7,8. Here is the secret of the backsliding of the Galatians, and of the trouble which so many find in living the Christian life. The Galatians began in the Spirit, but thought to attain to perfection by the flesh (chapter 3:3), a thing as impossible as to reach the stars by delving in the earth. So many people desire to do right, but, not having definitely and fully yielded to the Spirit, they can not do the things that they would. The Spirit strives with them, and has partial control, or is at times quite fully yielded to, and they have a rich experience; then the Spirit is grieved, the flesh asserts itself, and they seem like other persons. They are swayed at times by the mind of the Spirit, and at times by the mind of the flesh (Rom. 8:6), and so, being double-minded, they are unstable in all their ways (Jam. 1:8). It is a most unsatisfactory position in which to be. {224}

The Spirit and the Law

"If ye be led of the Spirit, ye are not under the law." "For we know that the law is spiritual; but I am carnal, sold under sin." Rom. 7:14. The flesh and the Spirit are in opposition; but against the fruits of the Spirit there is no law. Gal. 5:22,23. Therefore the law is against the works of the flesh. The carnal mind is "not subject to the law of God." So those who are in the flesh can not please God, but are "under the law." This is another clear proof of the fact that to be "under the law" is to be a transgressor of it. "The law is spiritual;" therefore all who are led by the Spirit are in full harmony with the law, and so they are not under it.

Here again we see that the controversy was not whether or not the law should be kept; that never at that time came into the mind of anybody professing godliness. But the question was concerning how it could be fulfilled. The Galatians were being led astray by the flattering teaching that they themselves had power to do it, while the heaven-sent apostle strenuously maintained that only through the Spirit could it be kept. This he showed from the Scriptures, from the history of Abraham, and from the experience of the Galatians themselves. They began in the Spirit, and as long as they continued in the Spirit, they ran well; but when they substituted themselves for the Spirit, immediately the works began to manifest themselves, which were wholly contrary to the law. The Holy Spirit is the life of God; God is love; love is the fulfilling of the law; the law is spiritual. Therefore whoever would be spiritual {225} must submit to the righteousness of God, which is witnessed to by the law, but is gained only through the faith of Jesus Christ. Whoever is led by the Spirit must keep the law, not as a condition of receiving the Spirit, but as the necessary result.

We often find people who profess to be so spiritual, so wholly led by the Spirit, that they do not need to keep the law. They admit that they do not keep the law, but say that it is the Spirit that leads them to do as they do, and that, therefore, it can not be sin, even though opposed to the law. Such persons make the terrible mistake of substituting their own carnal mind for the mind of the Spirit. They have confounded the flesh with the Spirit, and have thus put themselves in the place of God. That is the very worst kind of popery. To speak against the law of God, is to speak against the Spirit. They are terribly blinded, and should pray, "Open Thou mine eyes, that I may behold wondrous things out of Thy law."

The Fruit of the Spirit.

The first-fruit of the Spirit is love, and "love is the fulfilling of the law." Joy and peace come next, for, "being justified by faith, we have peace with God through our Lord Jesus Christ." "And not only so, but we also joy in God through our Lord Jesus Christ." Rom. 5:1,11. Christ was anointed with the Holy Ghost (Acts 10:38), or, as stated in another place, "with the oil of gladness" (Heb. 1:9). The service of God is a joyful service. The kingdom of God is "righteousness, and peace, and joy in the Holy Ghost." Rom. 14:17. He who is not glad, {226} not occasionally merely, but all the time,—glad in adversity as well as in prosperity,—does not yet know the Lord as he should. The words of Christ lead to fullness of joy. n 15:11.

Love, joy, peace, long-suffering, gentleness, goodness, faith, meekness, temperance, must come forth spontaneously from the heart of the true follower of Christ. They can not be forced. But they do not dwell naturally in us. It is natural for us to be angry and exasperated, instead of gentle and long-suffering, when opposed. Note the contrast between the works of the flesh and the fruits of the Spirit. The first come naturally; therefore, in order for the good fruit to be borne, we must be made completely over into new creatures. "A good man out of the good treasure of his heart bringeth forth that which is good." Luke 6:45. Goodness comes not from any man, but from the Spirit of Christ continually dwelling in him.

Christ's by Crucifixion

"They that are Christ's have crucified the flesh with the passions and lusts." It is by death that we become joined to Christ. As many as are baptized into Christ, have put on Christ (Gal. 5:27), and as many as have been baptized into Christ, have been baptized into His death (Rom. 6:3). "Our old man is crucified with Him, that the body of sin might be destroyed, that henceforth we should not serve sin. For he that is dead is freed from sin." Rom. 6:6,7. "I am crucified with Christ; nevertheless I live; yet not I, but Christ liveth in me; and the life which I now live in the flesh I live by the faith of the Son of God, {227} who loved me, and gave Himself for me." Gal. 2:20. This is the experience of every true child of God. "If any man be in Christ, he is a new creature." 2 Cor. 5:17. He still lives in the flesh, to all outward appearance the same as other men, yet he is in the Spirit, and not in the flesh. Rom. 8:9. He lives in the flesh a life that is not of the flesh, and the flesh has no power over him, but, so far as its works are concerned, is dead. "The body is dead because of sin; but the Spirit is life because of righteousness."

Walking in the Spirit

"If we live in the Spirit, let us also walk in the Spirit." Is there any doubt as to whether or not we live in the Spirit?—Not the slightest, nor is there any implied. Because we live in the Spirit, we are in duty bound to submit to the Spirit. Only by the Spirit's power—the same Spirit that in the beginning hovered over the face of the deep and brought order out of chaos—can any person live. "The Spirit of God hath made me, and the breath of the Almighty hath given me life." Job 33:4. By the same breath were the heavens made. Ps. 33:6. The Spirit of God is the life of the universe. The Spirit of God in our nostrils (Job 27:3) keeps us in life. The Spirit is the universal presence of God, in whom "we live, and move, and have our being." We are dependent on the Spirit for life, and therefore should walk according to, or be guided by, the Spirit. This is our "reasonable service."

What a wondrous possibility is here set forth! To live in the flesh as though the flesh were spirit. "There is a natural body, and there is a spiritual {228} body." "Howbeit that was not first which is spiritual, but that which is natural; and afterwards that which is spiritual." 1 Cor. 15:44,46. The natural body we now have; the spiritual body all the true followers of Christ will receive at the resurrection. See 1 Cor. 15:42–44,50–53. Yet in this life, in the natural body, men are to be spiritual,—to live just as they will in the future spiritual body. "Ye are not in the flesh, but in the Spirit, if so be that the Spirit of God dwell in you." Rom. 8:9. "The natural man receiveth not the things of the Spirit of God; for they are foolishness unto him; neither can he know them; because they are spiritually discerned. But he that is spiritual judgeth all things." 1 Cor. 2:14,15.

"Except a man be born again [from above], he can not see the kingdom of God." "That which is born of the flesh is flesh; and that which is born of the Spirit is spirit." n 3:3,6. By our natural birth we inherit all the evils enumerated in this fifth chapter of Galatians, "and such like." We are fleshly; corruption rules in us. By the new birth we inherit the fullness of God, being made "partakers of the Divine nature, having escaped the corruption that is in the world through lust." 2 Pet. 1:4. "The old man, which is corrupt according to the deceitful lusts" (Eph. 4:22), is crucified, and "put off," "that the body of sin might be destroyed, that henceforth we should not serve sin" (Rom. 6:6). Abiding in the Spirit, walking in the Spirit, the flesh with its lusts has no more power over us than if we were actually dead and in our graves. It is then the Spirit of God alone that animates the body. The Spirit uses the {229} flesh as an instrument of righteousness. The flesh is still corruptible, still full of lusts, still ready to rebel against the Spirit, but as long as we yield our wills to God, the Spirit holds the flesh in check. If we waver, if we in our hearts turn back to Egypt, or if we become self-confident, and so relax our dependence on the Spirit, then we build again the things that we destroyed, and again make ourselves transgressors. But this need not be. Christ has "power over all flesh," and He has demonstrated His ability to live a spiritual life in human flesh.

This is the Word made flesh, God manifest in the flesh. It is the revelation of "the love of Christ, which passeth knowledge, that we might be filled with all the fullness of God." With this Spirit of love and meekness ruling us, we shall not be desirous of vainglory, provoking one another, envying one another. All things will be of God, and this will be acknowledged, so that none will have any disposition to boast over another.

This Spirit of life in Christ—the life of Christ—is given freely to all. "Whosoever will, let him take the water of life freely." "For the Life was manifested, and we have seen it, and bear witness, and show unto you that eternal life, which was with the Father, and was manifested unto us." "Thanks be unto God for His unspeakable gift." {230}

The Glory Of The Cross

IN the last part of the fifth chapter, and in the sixth, we learn the practical character of the entire Epistle. Hasty readers are likely to think that there is a division in it, and that the latter part treats of practical, spiritual life, while the first part is devoted to theoretical doctrines. This is a great error. No part of the Bible is theory; it is all fact. There is no part of the Bible that is not spiritual and practical. Moreover, it is all doctrine. Doctrine means teaching. Christ's talk to the multitudes on the mount is called doctrine, because "He opened His mouth and taught them." Some people express a sort of contempt for doctrine; they speak slightingly of it, as though it belonged to the realm of abstruse theology, and not to practical, every-day life. Such ones unconsciously do dishonor to the preaching of Christ, which was nothing else but doctrine. That is to say, He always taught the people. All true doctrine is intensely practical; it is given to men for no other purpose than to be practiced.

Sermonizing Not Doctrine

People are led into this error by a wrong use of words. That which they call doctrine, and which they speak of as impractical, is not doctrine, but sermonizing. That is impractical, and {231} has no place in the Gospel. No preacher of the Gospel ever "delivers a sermon." If he does, it is because he chooses for a time to do something else besides preach the Gospel. Christ never delivered a sermon. Instead of that, He gave the people doctrine; that is to say, He taught them. He was "a Teacher sent from God." So the Gospel is all doctrine; it is instruction in the life of Christ.

The object of this Epistle is clearly seen in this closing portion. It is not to furnish ground for controversy, but to silence it by leading the readers to submit themselves to the Spirit, whose fruits are love, joy, peace, long-suffering, gentleness, goodness. Its purpose is to reclaim those who are sinning against God by "trying to serve" Him in their "own weak way," and to lead them to serve indeed "in newness of Spirit." All the so-called argument of the preceding portion of the Epistle is simply the demonstration of the fact that "the works of the flesh," which are sin, can be escaped only by the circumcision of the cross of Christ,—by serving God in Spirit, and having no confidence in the flesh.

"Brethren, even if a man be overtaken in any trespass, ye which are spiritual, restore such a one in a spirit of meekness; looking to thyself, lest thou also be tempted. Bear ye one another's burdens, and so fulfil the law of Christ. For if a man thinketh himself to be something, when he is nothing, he deceiveth himself. But let each man prove his own work, and then shall he have his glorying in regard of himself alone, and not of his neighbor. For each man shall bear his own burden. {232}

"But let him that is taught in the Word communicate unto him that teacheth in all good things. Be not deceived; God is not mocked; for whatsoever a man soweth, that shall he also reap. For he that soweth unto his own flesh shall of the flesh reap corruption; but he that soweth unto the Spirit shall of the Spirit reap eternal life. And let us not be weary in well-doing; for in due season we shall reap, if we faint not. So then, as we have opportunity, let us work that which is good toward all men, and especially toward them that are of the household of the faith.

"See with how large letters I have written unto you with mine own hand. As many as desire to make a fair show in the flesh, they compel you to be circumcised; only that they may not be persecuted for the cross of Christ. For not even they who receive circumcision do themselves keep the law; but they desire to have you circumcised, that they may glory in your flesh. But far be it from me to glory, save in the cross of our Lord Jesus Christ, through which the world hath been crucified unto me, and I unto the world. For neither is circumcision anything, nor uncircumcision, but a new creature. And as many as shall walk by this rule, peace be unto them, and mercy, and upon the Israel of God.

"From henceforth let no man trouble me; for I bear branded on my body the marks of Jesus.

"The grace of our Lord Jesus Christ be with your spirit, brethren. Amen." Galatians 6, R.V. {233}

A Radical Change

When men set out to make themselves righteous, pride, emulation, vainglory, boasting, criticism, fault-finding, and backbiting, leading to open quarrels, are the result. So it was with the Galatians, and so it will ever be. It can not be otherwise. Each individual has his own conception of the law,—for, having determined to be justified by the law, he reduces it to the level of his own mind, so that he may be judge,—and can not resist examining his brethren, as well as himself, to see if they are up to his measure. If his critical eye detects one who is not walking according to his rule, he at once proceeds to "deal with the offender," who, if humble submission—not to God, but to his judges—be not tendered, must be turned out of the church, lest the robes of "our righteousness" be defiled by contact with him. The self-righteous ones constitute themselves their brother's keeper, to the extent of keeping him out of their company, lest they should be disgraced. In marked contrast with this spirit, which is all too common in the church, is the exhortation with which this chapter opens. Instead of hunting for faults, that we may condemn them, we are to hunt for sinners, that we may save them.

"Sin Coucheth at the Door"

To Cain God said, "If thou doest not well, sin coucheth at the door; and unto thee is its desire, but thou shouldest rule over it." Gen. 4:7, R.V., margin. Sin is a venomous beast, lurking in secret, watching every opportunity to spring upon {234} and overcome the unwary. Its desire is to us, but power has been given us to rule over it. "Let not sin therefore reign in your mortal body." Nevertheless it is possible (not necessary) for the most zealous ones to be overtaken. "These things write I unto you, that ye may sin not. And if any man sin, we have a Comforter with the Father, Jesus Christ the Righteous; and He is the propitiation for our sins; and not for ours only, but also for the whole world." 1 n. 2:1,2, R.V., margin. So, even though a man be overtaken in any trespass, he is to be restored, and not thrust further away.

The Gospel Means Restoration

"For the Son of man is come to save that which was lost. How think ye? if a man have an hundred sheep, and one of them be gone astray, doth he not leave the ninety and nine, and goeth into the mountains, and seeketh that which is gone astray? And if so be that he find it, verily I say unto you, he rejoiceth more of that sheep, than of the ninety and nine which went not astray. Even so it is not the will of your Father which is in heaven, that one of these little ones should perish." Matt. 18:11–14. Christ is now in the heavens "until the times of restoration of all things."

Save the One

The Lord represents His work by the case of the shepherd who seeks after the one sheep that has gone astray. The work of the Gospel is an individual work. Even though under the preaching of the Gospel thousands accept it in one day, as the result of one discourse, it {235} is because of its effect on each individual heart. When the preacher, in speaking to thousands, addresses each one individually, then he is doing the work of Christ. So if a man be overtaken in a fault, restore such an one, in the spirit of meekness. No man's time is so precious that it is wasted when devoted to the salvation of one single person. Some of the most important and glorious truths that we have on record as uttered by Christ, were addressed to only one listener. He who looks after and cares for the single lambs of the flock, is a good shepherd.

The Ministry of Reconciliation

"God was in Christ, reconciling the world unto Himself, not imputing their trespasses unto them; and hath committed unto [put into] us the word of reconciliation." 2 Cor. 5:19. He "His own self bare our sins in His own body." 1 Pet. 2:24. He did not impute our trespasses to us, but took them all on Himself. "A soft answer turneth away wrath." Christ comes to us with gentle words, not harshly chiding us, in order that He may win us. He calls us to come to Him and find rest; to exchange our galling yoke of bondage, and heavy burden, for His easy yoke and light burden.

In Christ's Stead

All Christians are one in Christ. There is but one seed—all are embraced in Christ, the Representative Man. Therefore "as He is, so are we in this world." 1 . 4:17. Christ was in this world as an example of what men ought to be, and of what His true followers will be when wholly consecrated {236} to Him. To His disciples He says, "As My Father hath sent Me, even so send I you," and to this end He clothes them with His own power through the Spirit. "God sent not His Son into the world to condemn the world; but that the world through Him might be saved." n 3:17. Therefore we are not sent to condemn, but to save. Hence the injunction, "If a man be overtaken in a fault,...restore such an one." This is not to be limited to those who are associated with us in church capacity. We are sent as ambassadors for Christ, to beseech men, in Christ's stead, to be reconciled to God. 2 Cor. 5:20. The whole universe provides no greater work; no higher office can be found in heaven or earth than that of ambassador for Christ, which is the office of even the lowliest and most despised soul that is reconciled to God.

"Ye Which Are Spiritual"

Only such ones are called upon to restore the erring; none others can do it. The Holy Spirit alone must speak through those who would reprove and rebuke. It is Christ's own work that is to be done, and only by the power of the Spirit can anybody be a witness to Him. But would it, then, not be great presumption for anybody to go to restore a brother? Would it not be as much as claiming that he himself is spiritual? It is indeed no light matter to stand in Christ's place to any fallen man; and the design of God is that each one should take heed to himself, "considering thyself lest thou also be tempted." It is plain that the rule here laid down is calculated to work a revival in the church. {237}

As soon as a man is overtaken in a fault, the duty of each one is—not straightway to talk to somebody about him, nor even to go directly to the erring one himself, but—to ask himself, How do I stand? Am I not guilty, if not of the same thing, of something equally bad? May it not even be that some fault in me has led to his fall? Am I walking in the Spirit, so that I could restore him, and not drive him further away? This would result in a complete reformation in the church, and it might well be that by the time the others had got into condition to go to the faulty one, he might also have recovered himself from the snare of the devil.

Bound in Heaven

In giving directions how to deal with one who has committed a trespass (Matt. 18:10–18), the Saviour said, "Verily I say unto you, Whatsoever ye shall bind on earth shall be bound in heaven; and whatsoever ye shall loose on earth shall be loosed in heaven." Does this mean that God pledges Himself to be bound by any decision that any company of men calling themselves His church may make?—Certainly not. Nothing that is done on earth can change God's will. The history of the church, as we have it for nearly eighteen hundred years, is a record of mistakes and errors, of self-aggrandizement, and of putting self in the place of God. Who can read the history of the councils of the church, and say that God was in any of them, or that He either prompted or sanctioned any of their decrees?

What, then, did Christ mean?—Just what He said. His instruction shows that He meant that the church {238} should be spiritual,—filled with the spirit of meekness,—and that every one who spoke should "speak as the oracles of God." Only the Word of Christ should be in the heart and mouth of all who deal with a trespasser. When this is the case, it follows, since God's Word is settled forever in heaven, that whatever is bound on earth must necessarily be bound in heaven. But this will not be the case unless the Scriptures are strictly followed in letter and in spirit.

"The Law of Christ"

This is fulfilled by bearing one another's burdens, because the law of Christ's life is to bear burdens. "All we like sheep have gone astray; we have turned every one to his own way; and the Lord hath laid on Him the iniquity of us all." Is. 53:6. "Surely He hath borne our griefs, and carried our sorrows." Whoever would fulfil His law must have His life in him, still doing the same work for the strayed and fallen.

"In all things it behooved Him to be made like unto His brethren, that He might be a merciful and faithful High Priest in things pertaining to God, to make reconciliation for the sins of the people. For in that He Himself hath suffered being tempted, He is able to succor them that are tempted." Heb. 2:17,18. He knows what it is to be sorely tempted, and He knows how to overcome. Yea, although He "knew no sin," He was made even to be sin for us, that we might be made the righteousness of God in Him. 2 Cor. 5:21. He took every one of our sins, and confessed them before God as His own. Even so He comes to us. Instead of upbraiding us for {239} our sin, He opens His heart to us, and tells us how He has suffered with the same infirmity, and that He knows all the hardship, the pain, the sorrow, and the shame. Thus He draws us to Himself, and wins our confidence. Knowing that He has passed through the same experience, that He has been down into the very depths, we are ready to listen to Him when He talks about the way of escape. We know that He is talking from experience.

The greatest part, therefore, of the work of saving sinners is to show ourselves one with them. That is to say, it is in the confession of our own faults that we save others. The man who feels himself without sin, is not the man to restore the sinful. He who goes to one who is overtaken in any trespass, and says, "How in the world could you ever do such a thing? I never did a thing like that in my life, and I can't see how anybody with any sense of self-respect could do so," might far better stay at home. God chose one Pharisee, and only one, to be an apostle, but he was not sent forth until he could acknowledge himself to be the chief of sinners. 1 Tim. 1:15. It is humiliating to confess sin. That is true, but the way of salvation is the way of the cross. It was only by the cross that Christ could be the Saviour of sinners. Therefore if we would share His joy, we must with Him endure the cross, despising the shame. Remember this fact: It is only by confessing our own sins that we can save others from their sins. Only thus can we show them the way of salvation; for it is he who confesses his sins that obtains cleansing from them, and so can lead others to the fountain. {240}

Man Is Nothing

"If a man thinketh himself to be something, when he is nothing, he deceiveth himself." Mark those words, "when he is nothing." It does not say that we should not think ourselves to be something until we are something. No; it is a statement of the fact that we are nothing. Not merely a single individual, but all nations, are nothing before the Lord. If we ever at any time think ourselves to be something, we deceive ourselves. And we often do deceive ourselves, and thus mar the work of the Lord. Remember the law of Christ. Although He was everything, He emptied Himself. He obliterated Himself, that the work of God might be done. "The servant is not greater than his lord." God alone is great; "every man at his best state is altogether vanity." God alone is true, but every man a liar. When we acknowledge this, and live in consciousness of it, then we are where the Spirit of God can fill us, and then God can work through us. The "man of sin" is he that exalteth himself. 2Thess. 2:3,4. The child of God is the one who humbles himself.

Bear Your Own Burdens

"For every man shall bear his own burden." Is this a contradiction of verse 2?—By no means. When the Scripture tells us to bear one another's burdens, it does not tell us to throw our burdens on one another. Each one is to cast his burden on the Lord. Ps. 55:22. He bears the burden of the whole world, of all mankind, not in mass, but for each individual. We cast our burdens on Him, not {241} by gathering them up in our hands, or with our mind, and hurling them from ourselves to one who is at a distance. That can never be done. Many have tried to get rid of their burden of sin and pain and care and sorrow, but have failed, and have felt it roll back upon their own heads heavier than ever, until they have well-nigh sunk in despair. What was the trouble?—Simply this: they regarded Christ as at a distance from them, and they felt that they themselves must bridge the gulf. It is impossible. The man who is "without strength" can not cast his burden the length of his arm, and as long as we keep the Lord at arm's length, we shall not know rest from the weary load. It is when we recognize and confess Him in us, as our sole support, our life, the One whose power it is that makes every motion, and so confess that we are nothing, and sink out of sight, no longer deceiving ourselves, that we leave the burden resting on Christ. He knows what to do with it, and yoking up with Him we learn of Him how to bear the burdens of others.

Then how about bearing our own burden?—Ah, it is the Divine "power that worketh in us" that bears it! "I am crucified with Christ; nevertheless I live; yet not I, but Christ liveth in me." It is I, and yet it is not I, but Christ. Now I have learned the secret. I will not weary somebody else with the story of my burden, but will bear it myself, yet not I, but Christ in me. There are people enough in the world who have not yet learned this lesson of Christ, so that every child of God will always find work to do in bearing burdens for others; his own he will {242} entrust to the Lord, to find whom he has no further to go than to his own heart. Is it not blessed to have "One who is mighty" always under the burden which falls upon our shoulders?

This lesson we learn from the life of Christ. He went about doing good, for God was with Him. He comforted the mourners, He bound up the broken-hearted, He healed all that were oppressed of the devil. Not one who came to Him with a tale of sorrow or a distressing malady was turned away without relief; "that it might be fulfilled which was spoken by Esaias the prophet, saying, Himself took our infirmities, and bare our sicknesses." Matt. 8:17. And then when night sent the multitude to their beds, He sought the mountain or the forest, that in communion with the Father, by whom He lived, He might find a fresh supply of life and strength for His own soul. "Let every man prove his own work." "Examine yourselves, whether ye be in the faith; prove your own selves. Know ye not your own selves, how that Jesus Christ is in you, except ye be reprobates?" 2 Cor. 13:5. "Though He was crucified through weakness, yet He liveth by the power of God. For we also are weak with Him, but we shall live with Him by the power of God." Verse 4, margin. So if our faith proves to us that Christ is in us,—and faith proves to us the reality of the fact,—we have rejoicing in ourselves alone, and not in another. We joy in God through our Lord Jesus Christ, and our joy does not depend upon any {243} other person in the world. Though all should fail and be discouraged, we can stand, for the foundation of God—Christ— standeth sure.

Therefore let no one who calls himself a Christian be content to lean on somebody else, but let him, though he be the weakest of the weak, be a burden-bearer,—a worker together with God,—in Christ bearing quietly and uncomplainingly his own burdens, and those of his neighbors also. He can discover some of the burdens of his uncomplaining brother, and bear them, and the other will do likewise. So the rejoicing of the weak will be, "The Lord Jehovah is my strength and my song; He also is become my salvation."

Communicating Good Things

"Let him that is taught in the Word communicate unto him that teacheth in all good things." There can be no doubt but that this refers primarily to temporal support. "The laborer is worthy of his hire." If a man gives himself wholly to the ministry of the Word, it is evident that the things necessary for his sustenance must come from those who are taught. But this by no means exhausts the meaning of the injunction. The one who is taught in the Word must communicate to the teacher "in all good things." Mutual help is the burden of this chapter. "Bear ye one another's burdens." Even the teacher who is supported by those who are taught, is to assist others pecuniarily. Christ and the apostles, who had nothing of their own—for Christ was the poorest of the poor, and the disciples had left {244} all to follow Him—nevertheless distributed to the poor out of their little store. See n 13:29.

When the disciples told Jesus to send the hungry multitudes away, that they might buy themselves victuals, He said, "They need not depart; give ye them to eat." Matt. 14:16. He was not trifling with them; He meant what He said. He knew that they had nothing to give the people, but they had as much as He had. They did not perceive the power of His words, so He Himself took the few loaves and dealt out to the disciples, and thus they did really feed the hungry people. But His words to them meant that they should do just what He did. How many times our own lack of faith in Christ's Word has hindered us from doing good and communicating (Heb. 13:16), the sacrifices which please God.

As the teachers contribute not only the Word but temporal support as well, so those who are taught in the Word should not confine their liberality merely to temporal things. It is a mistake to suppose that ministers of the Gospel never stand in need of spiritual refreshment, or that they can not receive it from the weakest in the flock. No one can ever tell how much the souls of teachers are encouraged by the testimonies of faith and joy in the Lord, which come from the mouths of those who have heard the Word. It is not simply that the teacher sees that his labor is not in vain. The testimony may have no reference whatever to anything that he has done; but a humble soul's joyful testimony to what God has done for him, will often, through the refreshment it gives the teacher of the Word, be the means of strengthening the souls of hundreds. {245}

Sowing and Reaping

"Whatsoever a man soweth, that shall he also reap." A simple statement of fact, that can not be made plainer by any amount of talk. The harvest, which is the end of the world, will reveal what the sowing has been, whether wheat or tares. "He that soweth to his flesh shall of the flesh reap corruption; but he that soweth to the Spirit shall of the Spirit reap life everlasting." "Sow to yourselves in righteousness, reap in mercy; break up your fallow ground; for it is time to seek the Lord, till He come and rain righteousness upon you." Hos. 10:12. "He that trusteth in his own heart is a fool," and equally foolish is he who trusts in other men, as is seen from the next verse: "Ye have plowed wickedness, ye have reaped iniquity; ye have eaten the fruit of lies; because thou didst trust in thy way, in the multitude of mighty men." "Cursed be the man that trusteth in man, and maketh flesh his arm," whether it be his own flesh or that of some other man. "Blessed is the man that trusteth in the Lord, and whose hope the Lord is." Jer. 17:5,7.

Everything enduring comes from the Spirit. The flesh is corrupt, and it corrupts. He who consults only his own pleasure,—fulfilling the desires of the flesh and of the mind,—will reap a harvest of corruption and death. But "the Spirit is life because of righteousness," and he who consults only the mind of the Spirit, will reap everlasting glory; for "if the Spirit of Him that raised up Jesus from the dead dwell in you, He that raised up Christ from the dead shall also quicken your mortal bodies by His Spirit {246} that dwelleth in you." "For if ye live after the flesh, ye shall die; but if ye through the Spirit do mortify the deeds of the body, ye shall live." Rom. 8:11,13. Wonderful! If we live, we die; if we die, we live! This is the testimony of Jesus: "Whosoever will save his life shall lose it; and whosoever will lose his life for My sake shall find it." Matt. 16:25.

This does not mean the loss of all joy in this present time. It does not mean undergoing a continual deprivation and penance, going without something that we long for, for the sake of getting something else by and by. It does not mean that life in this present time shall be a living death, a long-drawn-out agony. Far from it. That is a crude and false idea of the Christian life—the life that is found in death. No; whoever comes to Christ and drinks of the Spirit, has in himself "a well of water springing up into everlasting life." n 4:14. The joy of eternity is his now. His joy is full day by day. He is abundantly satisfied with the fatness of God's house, drinking of the river of God's own pleasure. He has all that he longs for, because his heart and his flesh cry out only for God, in whom is all fullness. Once he though he was "seeing life," but now he knows that he was then but gazing into the grave, the pit of corruption. Now he begins really to live, and the joy of the new life is "unspeakable, and full of glory." So he sings:—

> *"Now none but Christ can satisfy,*
> *None other name for me;*
> *There's love, and life, and lasting joy,*
> *Lord Jesus, found in Thee."* {247}

A shrewd general always seeks to seize upon the strongest positions; so wherever there is a rich promise to believers, Satan tries to distort it, so as to make it a source of discouragement. Accordingly, he has made many believe that the words, "He that soweth to his flesh shall of the flesh reap corruption," mean that they must all their lives, even after being born of the Spirit, suffer the consequences of their former life of sin. Some have supposed that even in eternity they would have to bear the scars of their old sins, saying, "I can never hope to be what I should have been if I had never sinned."

What a libel on God's mercy, and the redemption that is in Christ Jesus! That is not the freedom wherewith Christ makes us free. The exhortation is, "As ye have yielded your members servants to uncleanness and to iniquity unto iniquity; even so now yield your members servants to righteousness unto holiness;" but if the one who thus yields himself to righteousness must always be handicapped by his former bad habits, that would prove that the power of righteousness is less than that of sin. But that is not so. Grace abounds over sin, and is as mighty as the heavens.

Here is a man who for gross crimes has been condemned to imprisonment for life. After a few years' imprisonment he receives a free pardon, and is set at liberty. Some time afterward we meet him, and see a fifty-pound cannon-ball attached to his leg by a huge chain, so that he can move about only with the greatest difficulty. "Why, how is this?" we ask in surprise. "Were you not given your freedom?" "Oh, {248} yes," he replies, "I am free; but I have to wear this ball and chain as a reminder of my former crimes." One would not think of such "freedom" as that very desirable.

Every prayer inspired by the Holy Ghost is a promise of God; and one of the most gracious of these is this: "Remember not the sins of my youth, nor my transgressions; according to Thy mercy remember Thou me for Thy goodness' sake, O Lord." Ps. 25:7. When God forgives our sins, and forgets them, He gives us such power to escape from them that we shall be as though we had never sinned. By the "exceeding great and precious promises," we are made "partakers of the Divine nature, having escaped the corruption that is in the world through lust." 2 Pet. 1:4. Man fell by partaking of the tree of knowledge of good and evil; the Gospel presents such a redemption from the fall, that all the black memories of sin are effaced, and the redeemed ones come to know only the good, like Christ, "who knew no sin."

Yes; they that sow to the flesh shall of the flesh reap corruption, as we have all proved in ourselves. "But ye are not in the flesh, but in the Spirit, if so be that the Spirit of God dwell in you." The Spirit has power to free us from the sins of the flesh, and from all their consequences. Christ "loved the church, and gave Himself for it; that He might sanctify and cleanse it with the washing of water by the Word, that He might present it to Himself a glorious church, not having spot, or wrinkle, or any such thing; but that it should be holy and without blemish." {249}

Eph. 5:25–27. "By His stripes we are healed." The memory of sin,—not of individual sins,—will be perpetuated in eternity only by the scars in the hands and feet and side of Christ, which are the seal of our perfect redemption.

Be Not Weary

How naturally the exhortation follows, "Let us not be weary in well-doing; for in due season we shall reap, if we faint not." It is so easy for us to get tired doing good, that is, when we are not looking to Jesus. We like to have little intermissions, because constant doing good seems too much of a strain. But that is only when we have not fully learned the joy of the Lord, which is the strength that enables us to keep from getting weary. "They that wait upon the Lord shall renew their strength; they shall mount up with wings as eagles; they shall run, and not be weary; they shall walk, and not faint." Is. 40:31.

But that which is especially referred to here, as the context shows, is not simply the resisting of temptation in our own flesh, but the helping of others. Here we need to learn a lesson from Christ, who "shall not fail nor be discouraged till He have set judgment in the earth." Though nine out of ten whom He relieved never showed the least sign of appreciation, it made no difference with Him. He came to do good, and not to be appreciated. Therefore, "in the morning sow thy seed, and in the evening withhold not thine hand; for thou knowest not whether shall prosper, either this or that, or whether they both shall be alike good." Ecc. 11:6. We can {250} not tell how much we shall reap, nor from which of the seed that we sow. Some may fall by the wayside, and be snatched away before it has time to take root, and other may fall on stony ground, where it will wither, and still other may fall among thorns, and be choked; but one thing is certain, and that is that we shall reap. We do not know whether the morning sowing or the evening sowing will prosper, or whether both shall alike be good; but there is no possibility that both can be bad. One or the other alone may prosper, or else both may be good. Isn't that encouragement enough for us not to be weary in well-doing? The ground may seem poor, and the season may not be favorable, so that the prospect for a crop may be most unpromising, and we may be tempted to think that all our labor is wasted. Not so; "in due season we shall reap, if we faint not." "Therefore, my beloved brethren, be ye steadfast, unmovable, always abounding in the work of the Lord, forasmuch as ye know that your labor is not in vain in the Lord." 1 Cor. 15:58.

Make No Difference

"As we have therefore opportunity, let us do good unto all men, especially unto them who are of the household of faith." In this we see that the apostle speaks of temporal help, for it needs no special exhortation to preach the Word to those who are not of the household of faith; they are the ones to whom it is specially to be preached; but there is a natural tendency—natural, I say, not spiritual—to limit charities to those who are called "deserving." We hear much about "the worthy poor." But we are all unworthy {251} of the least of God's blessings, yet He showers them upon us continually. "If ye do good to them which do good to you, what thank have ye? for sinners also do even the same. And if ye lend to them of whom ye hope to receive, what thank have ye? for sinners also lend to sinners, to receive as much again. But love ye your enemies, and do good, and lend, hoping for nothing again; and your reward shall be great, and ye shall be the children of the Highest; for He is kind unto the unthankful and to the evil."

Seek the Opportunity

Note especially the beginning of the tenth verse. "As we have therefore opportunity," let us do good unto all men. Doing good to others is to be considered a privilege to be enjoyed, and not an irksome duty to be discharged. Men do not speak of disagreeable things as opportunities. No one says that he had an opportunity to injure himself, or that he had an opportunity to lose some money. On the contrary, a man will speak of an opportunity to make some money, or to escape from some threatened danger. It is thus that we are to consider doing good to the needy. But opportunities are always sought for. Men are always on the lookout for an opportunity to get gain. So the apostle teaches us that we should be seeking opportunities to help some one. This Christ did. He "went about doing good." He traveled about the country on foot, searching opportunities to do somebody some good, and He found them. He did good, "for God was with Him." His name is Immanuel, which means, "God with us." Now, as He is with us all the days, even to the end of {252} the world, so God is with us, doing good to us, that we also may do good. "We then, as workers together with Him, beseech you also that ye receive not the grace of God in vain." To this end, "receive ye the Holy Ghost."

Closing Words

We come now to the close of this most wonderful letter. Even as the whole of the Gospel is contained in the greeting, so we find it in the end. The apostle literally knew nothing else save Jesus Christ and Him crucified. He could not greet his friends without mentioning it. In every chapter of this Epistle, but especially in the last two, do we see how directly it is addressed to us. Everybody uses verses 1, 7–10 as applicable now, without any thought of the Galatians; but just as surely as these verses mean us, just the same as though the Galatians had never lived, so does the entire Epistle.

The consuming zeal of the apostle Paul in writing it is seen in the fact that, contrary to his usual custom, he seized the pen and wrote the Epistle with his own hand. Verse 11. As intimated in chapter 4, the apostle suffered from weak eyes, which hindered him much in his work, or would have hindered him but for the power of God resting on him; so that it was necessary for him always to have some one with him, to minister unto him, and to serve as amanuensis. From the Second Epistle to the Thessalonians (chapter 2:2) we learn that some took advantage of this fact to write letters to the churches in Paul's name, which troubled the brethren; but in the close of that Epistle (chapter 3:16–18) Paul indicated to {253} them how they might know an epistle that came from him. No matter by whom the body of it was written, he wrote the salutation and the signature with his own hand. So great was the urgency in this case, however, that he wrote the entire Epistle himself.

Only a Show

We can not deceive God, and it is useless to deceive ourselves or others. "The Lord seeth not as man seeth; for man looketh on the outward appearance, but the Lord looketh on the heart." 1 Sam. 16:7. The circumcision in which the "false brethren" were seeking to induce the Galatians to trust, meant self-righteousness, instead of righteousness by faith. They had the law only as "the form of righteousness and of truth." With their works they could make "a fair show in the flesh," but it was only an empty show; there was no reality in it. They could seem righteous without suffering persecution for the cross of Christ.

They did not indeed keep the law; not by any means; for the flesh is opposed to the law of the Spirit, and "they that are in the flesh can not please God." But they desired converts to "our faith," as so many call the particular theories which they hold. Christ said, "Woe unto you, scribes and Pharisees, hypocrites! for ye compass sea and land to make one proselyte, and when he is made, ye make him twofold more the child of hell than yourselves." Matt. 23:15. Such teachers glory in the flesh of their "converts." If they can count so many as belonging to "our denomination," so much "gain" in the past year, they feel virtuously happy. Numbers and appearances {254} count for much with men, but for nothing with God.

Real and Lasting Glory

"God forbid that I should glory save in the cross of our Lord Jesus Christ." Why glory in the cross?—Because by it the world is crucified to us, and we to the world. The Epistle ends where it begins,—with deliverance from "this present evil world," and it is the cross alone that accomplishes the deliverance. The cross is the symbol of humiliation, therefore we glory in it, because in humility is exaltation.

God Revealed in the Cross

Read the words of the Lord by the mouth of Jeremiah: "Let not the wise man glory in his wisdom, neither let the mighty man glory in his might, let not the rich man glory in his riches." Jer. 9:23.

Why should not the wise man glory in his wisdom?—Because so far as it is his own wisdom, it is foolishness. "The wisdom of this world is foolishness with God." "The Lord knoweth the thoughts of the wise, that they are vain." 1 Cor. 3:19,20. No man has any wisdom in which to glory, for his own wisdom is foolishness, and wisdom which God gives is something to cause humility instead of pride.

What about might? "All flesh is grass." Is. 40:6. "Every man at his best state is altogether vanity." Ps. 39:5. "Men of low degree are vanity, and men of high degree are a lie; to be laid in the balance, they are altogether lighter than vanity." But "power belongeth unto God." Ps. 62:9,11. {255}

As to riches, they are "uncertain." 1 Tim. 6:17. Man "heapeth up riches, and knoweth not who shall gather them." "Riches certainly make themselves wings; they fly away as an eagle toward heaven." Prov. 23:5. Only in Christ are found unsearchable and abiding riches.

Man, therefore, has absolutely nothing in which to boast, for what is there left of a man when he has nothing that can be called wealth, no wisdom whatever, and absolutely no strength? Everything that man is or has comes from the Lord. Therefore it is that he that glorieth is to glory in the Lord. 1 Cor. 1:31.

Now put this text with Gal. 6:14. The same Spirit inspired them both, so that there is no contradiction. One text says that we are to glory only in the knowledge of the Lord; the other says that there is nothing in which to glory save the cross of our Lord Jesus Christ. The conclusion, therefore, is that in the cross we find the knowledge of God. To know God is eternal life, and there is no life for mankind except through the cross of Christ. So again we see most clearly that all that may be known of God is revealed in the cross. Aside from the cross, there is no knowledge of God.

This shows us again that the cross is seen in all creation, for the everlasting power and divinity of God, even all that may be known of Him, are seen in the things that He has made. The power of God is seen in the things that are made, and the cross is the power of God. 1 Cor. 1:18. Out of weakness God brings strength; He saves men by death, so that even {256} the dead may rest in hope. No man can be so poor, so weak and sinful, so degraded and despised, that he may not glory in the cross. The cross takes him just where he is, for it is the symbol of shame and degradation, and reveals the power of God in him, and in that there is ground for everlasting glory.

The Cross Crucifies

The cross cuts us off from the world. Glory! for then it unites us to God, because the friendship of the world is enmity with God; "whosoever therefore will be a friend of the world is the enemy of God." Jam. 4:4. Through His cross Christ has destroyed the enmity. Eph. 2:15,16. "And the world passeth away, and the lust thereof; but he that doeth the will of God abideth forever." Then let the world pass away.

> "Fade, fade, each earthly joy,
> Jesus is mine;
> Break every tender tie,
> Jesus is mine.
> Dark is the wilderness;
> Earth has no resting-place;
> Jesus alone can bless;
> Jesus is mine."

The Cross Elevates

Jesus said, "I, if I be lifted up from the earth, will draw all men unto Me." This He said signifying what death He should die, namely, the death of the cross. He humbled Himself to death, even the death of the cross; "wherefore God also hath highly exalted Him, and given Him a name which is above every name." Phil. 2:8,9. He descended "first into the lower {257} parts of the earth. He that descended is the same also that ascended up far above all heavens, that He might fill all things." Eph. 4:9,10. It was through death that He ascended to the right hand of the Majesty in the heavens. It was the cross that lifted Him up from earth to heaven. Therefore it is the cross alone that brings us glory, and so it is the only thing in which to glory. The cross, which means derision and shame from the world, lifts us away from this world, and sets us with Christ in the heavenly places; and the power by which it does this is "the power that worketh in us," even the power that works in and upholds all things in the universe.

The Cross Creates

"For in Christ Jesus neither circumcision availeth anything, nor uncircumcision, but a new creature." That is, neither circumcision nor uncircumcision has any power. Salvation does not come from man, whatever his state or condition, or whatever he may do. In an uncircumcised state he is lost, and if he be circumcised he is no nearer salvation. Only the cross has power to save. The only thing that is of any value is a new creature, or, as indicated in the margin of the Revision, "a new creation." "If any man be in Christ, there is a new creation;" and it is only through death that we become joined to Him. Rom. 6:3.

> "Nothing in my hand I bring;
> Simply to Thy cross I cling"

The cross makes a new creation, so that here again we see a reason for glorying in it; for when the new {258} creation came from the hand of God in the beginning, "the morning stars sang together, and all the sons of God shouted for joy." Job 38:7.

The Sign of the Cross

Put together all the texts that we have read, which show: (1) That the cross of Christ is the only thing in which to glory; (2) that whoever glories must glory only in the knowledge of God; (3) that God hath chosen the weak things of the world to confound the mighty, so that none might glory save in Him; and, (4) that God is revealed in the things that He has made, and that creation, which manifests God's power, also presents the cross, because the cross of Christ is the power of God, and God is made known by it. What have we?—This, that the power it took to create the world, and all things that are in it,—the power that is exerted to keep all things in existence,—is the power that saves those who trust in it. This is the power of the cross.

So the power of the cross, by which alone salvation comes, is the power that creates, and that continues to work in all creation. But when God creates a thing, it is "very good;" so in Christ, in His cross, there is "a new creation." "We are His workmanship, created in Christ Jesus for good works, which God afore prepared that we should walk in them." Eph. 2:10, R.V. It is in the cross that this new creation is wrought, for its power is the power by which "in the beginning God created the heavens and the earth." This is the power that keeps the earth from utter destruction under the curse; which brings about the {259} changing seasons,—seed-time and harvest,—and that will at last renew the face of the earth, so that "it shall blossom abundantly, and rejoice even with joy and singing; the glory of Lebanon shall be given unto it, the excellency of Carmel and Sharon; they shall see the glory of the Lord, and the excellency of our God."

"The works of the Lord are great, sought out of all them that have pleasure therein. His work is honorable and glorious; and His righteousness endureth forever. He hath made His wonderful works to be remembered; the Lord is gracious and full of compassion." Ps. 111:2–4.

Here we see that the wonderful works of God reveal His righteousness, and His grace and compassion as well. This is another evidence that His works reveal the cross of Christ, in which infinite love and mercy are centered.

But "He hath made His wonderful works to be remembered;" or, "He hath made a memorial for His wonderful works." Why does He wish men to remember and declare His mighty acts?— In order that they may not forget, but may trust in, His salvation. He would have men continually meditate on His works, that they may know the power of the cross. It is in the works of His hands that we triumph. Ps. 92:4. So when God had made the heavens and earth, and all their host, in six days, "He rested on the seventh day from all His work which He had made. And God blessed the seventh day, and sanctified it; because that in it He had rested from all His work which God created and made." Gen. 2:2,3. {260}

The cross conveys to us the knowledge of God, because it shows us His power as Creator. Through the cross we are crucified unto the world, and the world unto us; that is, by the cross we are sanctified. But sanctification is the work of God, not of man. Only His divine power can accomplish the great work. In the beginning God sanctified the Sabbath, as the crown of His creative work—the evidence that His work was finished, the seal of perfection, and therefore He says, "Moreover also I gave them My Sabbaths, to be a sign between Me and them, that they might know that I am the Lord that sanctify them." Eze. 20:12.

So we see that the Sabbath—the seventh day—is the true sign of the cross. It is the memorial of creation, and redemption is creation,—creation through the cross. In the cross we find the complete and perfect works of God, and are clothed with them. Crucified with Christ means the utter giving up of self, acknowledging that we are nothing, and trusting absolutely in Christ. In Him we rest; in Him we find the Sabbath. The cross takes us back to the beginning, into "that which was from the beginning." The resting upon the seventh day of the week is but the sign of the fact that in the perfect work of God, as seen in creation,—in the cross,—we find rest from sin.

"But it is difficult to keep the Sabbath; my business will suffer;" "I couldn't make a living and keep the Sabbath;" "It is so unpopular." Oh, yes; nobody ever said that it was a specially pleasing thing to be crucified! "Even Christ pleased not Himself." {261}

Read the fifty-third chapter of Isaiah. Christ was not very popular, and least so of all when He was crucified. The cross means death; but it means also the entrance into life. There is healing in Christ's wounds, blessing in the curse that He bore, life in the death that He suffered. Who dare say that he trusts Christ for everlasting life if he dare not trust Him for a few years or months or days of life in this world? Accept the Sabbath of the Lord, and you will find that it means the cross to a degree that you never before dreamed of, and therefore "a far more exceeding and eternal weight of glory."

Now say once more, and say it from the heart: "Far be it from me to glory, save in the cross of our Lord Jesus Christ, through which the world hath been crucified unto me, and I unto the world." If you can say that in truth, you will find tribulations and afflictions so easy that you can glory in them.

"Hallelujah, what a Saviour!"

The Glory

It is by the cross that everything is sustained, for "in Him all things hold together," and He does not exist in any other form than that of the crucified One. But for the cross, there would be universal death. Not a man could breathe, not a plant could grow, not a ray of light could shine from heaven, if it were not for the cross. Now "the heavens declare the glory of God; and the firmament showeth His handiwork." Ps. 19:1. They are some of the things that God has made. No pen can describe and no artist's brush can depict the wondrous glory of the heavens; yet {262} that glory is but the glory of the cross of Christ. This follows from the facts already learned, that the power of God is seen in the things that are made, and that the cross is the power of God. The glory of God is His power, for "the exceeding greatness of His power to usward" is seen in the resurrection of Jesus Christ from the dead (Eph. 1:19,20), and "Christ was raised up from the dead by the glory of the Father" (Rom. 6:4). It was for the suffering of death that Jesus was crowned with glory and honor. Heb. 2:9. So we see that all the glory of the innumerable stars, with their various colors, all the glory of the rainbow, the glory of the clouds gilded by the setting sun, the glory of the sea, and of blooming fields and green meadows, the glory of the spring-time and of the ripened harvest, the glory of the opening bud and the perfect fruit,—yea, all the glory that Christ has in heaven, as well as the glory that will be revealed in His saints when they shall "shine forth as the sun in the kingdom of their Father," even "as the stars forever and ever,"— is the glory of the cross. How can we ever think of glorying in anything else?

The Israel of God

"As many as walk according to this rule, peace be on them, and mercy, and upon the Israel of God." The rule of glory! what a grand rule to walk by! Are there two classes here mentioned?—No; that can not be, for the Epistle has been devoted to showing that all are one in Christ Jesus. "And ye are complete in Him, which is the Head of all principality and power; in whom also ye are circumcised {263} with the circumcision made without hands, in putting off the body of the sins of the flesh by the circumcision of Christ; buried with Him in baptism, wherein also ye are risen with Him through the faith of the operation of God, who hath raised Him from the dead. And you, being dead in your sins and the uncircumcision of your flesh, hath He quickened together with Him, having forgiven you all trespasses." Col. 2:10–13. "We are the circumcision, which worship God in the Spirit, and rejoice in Christ Jesus, and have no confidence in the flesh." Phil. 3:3. This circumcision constitutes us all the true Israel of God, for this is the victory over sin, and "Israel" means an overcomer. No longer are we "aliens from the commonwealth of Israel," "no more strangers and foreigners, but fellow-citizens with the saints, and of the household of God; and are built upon the foundation of the apostles and prophets, Jesus Christ Himself being the chief cornerstone." Eph. 2:12,19,20. So we shall join the throng that "shall come from the east and west, and shall sit down with Abraham, and Isaac, and Jacob, in the kingdom of heaven."

The Marks of Christ

"From henceforth let no man trouble me; for I bear in my body the marks of the Lord Jesus." The Greek word rendered "marks" is the plural of "stigma," which we have incorporated into our own language. It signifies shame and disgrace, even as of old it meant a mark branded into the body of a culprit, or of a recaptured runaway slave, to show to whom he belonged. Such are the marks of the cross of Christ. {264}

The marks of the cross were upon Paul. He had been crucified with Christ, and he carried the nail-prints. They were branded on his body. They marked him as the bond-servant, the slave of the Lord Jesus. Let no one, then, interfere with him; he was not the servant of men. He owed allegiance to Christ alone, who had bought him. Let no one seek to get him to serve man or the flesh, because Jesus had branded him with His mark, and he could serve no other. Moreover, let men beware how they sought to interfere with his liberty in Christ, or how they treated him, for his Master would surely protect His own. Have you those marks? Then you may glory in them, for such boasting is not vain, and will not make you vain.

Ah, what glory there is in the cross! All the glory of heaven is in that despised thing. Not in the figure of the cross, but in the cross itself. The world does not reckon it glory, but then it did not know the Son of God, and it does not know the Holy Spirit, because it can not see Him. May God open our eyes to see the glory, so that we may reckon things at their true value. May we consent to be crucified with Christ, that the cross may glorify us. In the cross of Christ there is salvation. In it is the power of God to keep us from falling, for it lifts us up from earth to heaven. In the cross there is the new creation, which God Himself pronounces "very good." In it is all the glory of the Father, and all the glory of the eternal ages. Therefore God forbid that we should glory save in the cross of our Lord Jesus {265} Christ, by which the world is crucified to us, and we unto the world.

> *"In the cross of Christ I glory,*
> *Towering o'er the wrecks of time;*
> *All the light of sacred story*
> *Gathers round its head sublime."*

Therefore—

> *"Since I, who was undone and lost,*
> *Have pardon through His name and Word;*
> *Forbid it, then, that I should boast,*
> *Save in the cross of Christ, my Lord."*
> *"Where'er I go, I'll tell the story*
> *Of the cross, of the cross;*
> *In nothing else my soul shall glory,*
> *Save the cross, save the cross;*
> *And this my constant theme shall be,*
> *Through time and in eternity,*
> *That Jesus tasted death for me,*
> *On the cross, on the cross."*

Other books by TEACH Services, Inc.

The Antichrist 666 *William Josiah Sutton*
Positive proof for Bible Believing People: Who the beast is; Who his image is; What the mark of the beast is; How to count the number of the beast. Edited by Roy Allan Anderson, D.D.

The Anti-Christ Exposed *Dan Jarrard*
A biblical and historical study of the counterfeit religious system which is against God and His people.

Art of Massage *John Harvey Kellogg*
A classic manual the learner and the practitioner will find enlightening. Its comprehensive coverage of the physiological effects of massage, as well as the human form. Particularly helpful are the detailed therapeutic massage procedures for specific health needs.

The Celtic Church in Britain *Leslie Hardinge*
This is an authoritative study of the beliefs and practice of the Celtic Church which at the same time holds much interest for the non-specialist, containing as it does fascinating descriptions of the life of the early Celtic Christians in their monastic walled villages modelled on the Old Testament cities of refuge. Their elaborate penitential discipline was based on Old Testament compensatory regulations. Obedience to the Scriptures led them to establish a remarkable theocracy based on the laws of the Pentateuch and including the keeping of the Seventh-day Sabbath.

Champions of Christianity *Ronald C. Thompson*
Champions of Christianity in Search of Truth will reveal the effects of the Counter Reformation against truth, including the efforts for truth undertaken by the Radical Reformation and the Great Revival.

Christian Faith & Religious Freedom *Olsen, V.N.*
The theological grounding provided in this book is an important antidote to the tendency of many to base their arguments on religious freedom and church/state issues on political or constitutional grounds. Dr. Olsen makes an important contribution to our thinking by making us face the theological bedrock of any Christian approach to these topics.

Convert's Catechism *Peter Geiermann*
The quoted statement on changing solemnity from Saturday to Sunday can be found in this reproduction.

Cooking With Natural Foods I *Muriel Beltz*
An ideal eating program for a preventive lifestyle, weight control and stress control. A program designed to give an alternative in the prevention and treatment of disease.

Country Life Something Better Cookbook
This cookbook was originally designed to be used as a reference book in local community vegetarian cooking schools given across the country. Persons interested in better education in general health principles, and wholesome vegetarian recipes will find this cookbook a treasure to read, use and share. Completely revised and updated.

Divine Prescription   *G. Paulien*
All of the principles of the Bible and the Spirit of Prophecy are designed to allow us to function in perfect harmony with God Himself. This book discusses the methods and means of healthful living. It deals with going back to First Things, and relying by faith upon the substances which God has established for our benefit.

Dove of Gold   *Leslie Hardinge*
This book approaches the vast subject of the Holy Spirit viewing His functions through illustrations He himself has selected as vehicles for the revelation of His character and work. As one observes the related aspects of the nature and function of the natural object used as a symbol, the work of the Holy Spirit will become clearer, and His disposition of concern and affection much more appealing.

From Eden to Eden   *J. H. Waggoner*
A most interesting study of the more important historic and prophetic portions of the Scriptures.

Garlic—Nature's Prescription   *C. Gary Hullquist, MD*
Garlic, the Lily of Legend, has today become the focus of modern medical research. Recognized for thousands of years for its amazing curative powers, this bulb is today not only known for its potent bouquet but is drawing the attention of the scientific world as a potential antibiotic, anticancer, antioxidant, anti-aging, anti-inflammatory...the list goes on and on.

Gospel In Creation   *E. J. Waggoner*
This book directs our wandering gaze to the open pages of God's created works as the expression of the gospel, the power of God to save from sin. Facsimile Reprint.

Healthful Living   *Ellen G. White*
Wherever this book has been received, it has been recognized as a veritable storehouse of seed thoughts relating to the great practical themes with which it deals. Facsimile Reprint.

Helps to Bible Study   *J. L. Shuler*
A Bible marking system which contains Bible studies covering twenty-eight topics including "The Second Coming," "The Seal of the Living God," "Bible Temperance," and "Christian in Dress." It is simple and practical in its approach, and will benefit all ages.

Hydrotherapy *Thomas/Dail*
Help your body overcome common diseases using hydrotherapy and simple home treatments.

The Illuminati 666 *William Josiah Sutton*
Find out about the Illuminati, its startling history, and how powerful it has become. Includes a study of the origins of false religions, and the forms they are taking today. Introduction by Roy Allan Anderson, D.D.

The Justified Walk *Frank Phillips*
Before you can rightly tackle a problem, you must first be able to clearly understand its nature. Before you can discuss it with others, you must first define your terms. In this book Elder Phillips makes clear how the plan of salvation works in our daily lives. Faith, Grace, Sin, Justification, Sanctification and Righteousness are made real and tangible.

Lessons On Faith *Jones & Waggoner*
This is a compilation of articles and sermons given in the 1890's by Jones and Waggoner on Righteousness By Faith.

Living the Life of Enoch *E. G. White*
We are to live the Enoch life! This is our commission. and this is a twofold work—to develop a character of righteousness by living a life of personal purity and pleading with God; to teach a lesson of godliness by kindly acts and warning and pleading with men.

National Sunday Law *A. T. Jones*
This book is a report of an argument made concerning the national Sunday bill that was introduced by Senator Blair in the fiftieth Congress.

Nehemiah—Restoring the Breach *E.G. White*
This collection of articles by Ellen White dealing with the work of Nehemiah provides leaders and people among the remnant church with study material to help prepare them for the outpouring of the latter rain.

Nutrition Workshop Guide *E. Hullquist*
Chock full of nutritional recipes, as well as lots of helpful nutritional tips for special situations, such as road trips, fast foods, etc.

Power of Prayer *E. G. White*
Prayer is our connection with God—our strength, our bridge to heaven! As we pray, the Holy Spirit Himself unites in our petitions and "maketh intercession for us." We are not alone in our battle of life; all heaven is on our side!

Preparation For Translation *Milton Crane*
This book is about YOUR preparation for translation. It is about YOUR plans to live without a mediator after probation closes. It is about God's plans for YOUR overcoming temptation NOW in anticipation of those events. It is about His plans for the renewing

of YOUR mind through the final atonement ministry of Jesus. Spanish editions.

Rome's Challenge *Catholic Mirror*
The pages of this brochure unfold to the reader one of the most glaringly conceivable contradictions existing between the practice and theory of the Protestant world, and unsusceptible of any rational solution, the theory claiming the Bible alone as the teacher.

The Sabbath *M. L. Andreasen*
Attacks upon the Sabbath throughout the ages have been numerous and persistent, and they have all been grounded upon human reasoning as as against the command of God. Men can see no reason why any other day than one commanded by God is not just as good. Men cannot see why one day in seven is not just as good as the seventh day. The answer, of course, is that the difference lies in God's command. It is at this point that man's reason sets aside a positive command of God. It is not merely a question of this or that day, but the greater question of obedience to God's command.

The Sanctuary & the 2300 Days *J. N. Andrews*
Those who have any interest in the past Advent movement, cannot be otherwise than deeply interested in the question of our disappointment. To examine this question with candor and fairness, and to set forth the reasons why their expectations were not realized is the object of this work.

Story of Daniel the Prophet *S. N. Haskell*
This book especially applicable to our day: points out the immediate future and in its simplicity will attract many who might not be inclined to read deep, argumentative works. Facsimile Reprint.

Story of the Seer of Patmos *S. N. Haskell*
The Book of Revelation pronounces a blessing upon everyone who reads it or hears it. Facsimile Reprint.

Studies in Daniel and Revelation *K. Ashbaugh*
A convenient handbook containing paraphrases of EG White's comments after each verse in the books of Daniel & Revelation.

Studies in the Book of Hebrews *E. J. Waggoner*
A series of studies given at the General Conference of 1897. The Bible studies that Elder Waggoner gave each day, are presented as live and full of hope for each Bible student today.

Swift Arrow *Josephine Cunnington Edwards*
A large family migrated over from Europe in the early 1700's and settled in Pennsylvania. After some time, one of the sons, Marcus Boylan, and his family decided to join others to travel and settle the frontier. Disaster struck when two young boys were stolen by Indians, one being Marcus' son George. This is a true account of

his life with this Indian tribe, his eventual escape and journey back home.

Truth Triumphant *B. G. Wilkinson*
The history of God's true Church from Ireland, to the Waldenses, the struggle to preserve the Bible and the pure doctrine of the apostles is disclosed. Facsimile Reprint.

Understanding the Body Organs *Celeste Lee*
Simply and concisely explains how the body organs function and how they relate to one another. Also includes the eight laws of health, explaining each one and sharing many benefits that will be derived from following the entire plan.

The Word Was Made Flesh *Ralph Larson*
This book is on the human nature of Christ, with a limited, rather specialized objective. Dr. Larson does not deal directly with the whole issue of Christ's human nature. He traces the understanding of this aspect of Christology within the Seventh-day Adventist church from 1852–1952, providing a fairly comprehensive survey of historical data.

To order any of the above titles, see your local bookstore.
However, if you are unable to locate any title,
call 800/673-3742